Adolescent Selves

Shannon R. Kenney

Adolescent Selves

Same-Sex and Cross-Sex Parent-Teen Relationships on Adolescent Psychological and Cognitive Well-Being

VDM Verlag Dr. Müller

Imprint

Bibliographic information by the German National Library: The German National Library lists this publication at the German National Bibliography; detailed bibliographic information is available on the Internet at http://dnb.d-nb.de.

Any brand names and product names mentioned in this book are subject to trademark, brand or patent protection and are trademarks or registered trademarks of their respective holders. The use of brand names, product names, common names, trade names, product descriptions etc. even without a particular marking in this works is in no way to be construed to mean that such names may be regarded as unrestricted in respect of trademark and brand protection legislation and could thus be used by anyone.

Cover image: www.purestockx.com

Publisher:
VDM Verlag Dr. Müller Aktiengesellschaft & Co. KG
Dudweiler Landstr. 125 a, 66123 Saarbrücken, Germany
Phone +49 681 9100-698, Fax +49 681 9100-988, Email: info@vdm-verlag.de

Produced in Germany by:
Schaltungsdienst Lange o.H.G., Zehrensdorfer Str. 11, 12277 Berlin, Germany
Books on Demand GmbH, Gutenbergring 53, 22848 Norderstedt, Germany

Impressum

Bibliografische Information der Deutschen Nationalbibliothek: Die Deutsche Nationalbibliothek verzeichnet diese Publikation in der Deutschen Nationalbibliografie; detaillierte bibliografische Daten sind im Internet über http://dnb.d-nb.de abrufbar.

Alle in diesem Buch genannten Marken und Produktnamen unterliegen warenzeichen-, marken- oder patentrechtlichem Schutz bzw. sind Warenzeichen oder eingetragene Warenzeichen der jeweiligen Inhaber. Die Wiedergabe von Marken, Produktnamen, Gebrauchsnamen, Handelsnamen, Warenbezeichnungen u.s.w. in diesem Werk berechtigt auch ohne besondere Kennzeichnung nicht zu der Annahme, dass solche Namen im Sinne der Warenzeichen- und Markenschutzgesetzgebung als frei zu betrachten wären und daher von jedermann benutzt werden dürften.

Coverbild: www.purestockx.com

Verlag: VDM Verlag Dr. Müller Aktiengesellschaft & Co. KG
Dudweiler Landstr. 125 a, D- 66123 Saarbrücken,
Telefon +49 681 9100-698, Telefax +49 681 9100-988, Email: info@vdm-verlag.de

Herstellung in Deutschland:
Schaltungsdienst Lange o.H.G., Zehrensdorfer Str. 11, D-12277 Berlin
Books on Demand GmbH, Gutenbergring 53, D-22848 Norderstedt

ISBN: 978-3-8364-3776-9

TABLE OF CONTENTS

	Page
Title Page	i
Table of Contents	ii-iii
List of Tables	iv
List of Figures and Graphs	v

Chapter One, Introduction
    1.1. Premise...1
    1.2. Objectives...2
    1.3. Structure of Analyses...6

Chapter Two, Theoretical Framework
    2.1. Theories of Parent-Adolescent Identification and Attachment.......8
    2.2. Social Cognitive Theory...11
    2.3. Social Capital Theory...14
    2.4. Theoretical Framework..17

Chapter Three, Background and Hypotheses
    3.1. Adolescent Identity Formation...18
    3.2. Adolescent Depressed Mood..19
    3.3. Parent-Adolescent Relationships and Adolescent Depressed Mood...........24
    3.4. Gender-Specific Sources of Adolescent Depressed Mood...........28
    3.5. Mediation of Self-Esteem...34
    3.6. Parent-Adolescent Relationships and Adolescent Self-Esteem...38
    3.7. Gender-Specific Sources of Adolescent Self-Esteem..................41
    3.8. Mediation of Academic Achievement..44
    3.9. Parent-Adolescent Relationships and Academic Achievement...46
    3.10. Gender-Specific Sources of Academic Achievement................48
    3.11. Secondary Analyses...52
    3.12. Longitudinal Analyses...73

Chapter Four, Data and Methods
    4.1. Data...75
    4.2. Variable Operationalization..76
    4.3. Analyses..87

Chapter Five, Results
    5.1. Descriptive Statistics..91

        5.2. Full Sample Cross-Sectional Regression Analyses 95
        5.3. Female and Male Cross-Sectional Analyses...107
        5.4. Interaction Regression Analyses..124
        5.5. Strength of Paired Correlation Z-Tests 128
        5.6. Longitudinal Regression Analyses 133

Chapter Six, Discussion
        6.1. Cross-Sectional Analyses..140
        6.2. Longitudinal Analyses 161

Chapter Seven, Conclusion
        7.1. Limitations 163
        7.2. Conclusion 165

REFERENCES 170

APPENDIX
        A. NIMH Symptoms of Depression...197
        B. Adolescent Depressed Mood Survey Statements..197
        C. Adolescent Self-Esteem Survey Statements 198
        D. Parental Educational Attainment Survey Statements......................................198
        E. Adolescent Participation in School Clubs Survey Statements 198
        F. Adolescent Participation in School Athletics Survey Statements 199

LIST OF TABLES

Table	Page

1. Means, Standard Deviations, and Zero-Order Correlations among Continuous Variables and T-Tests of Gender Differences 92

2. Frequencies for Ordinal and Nominal Variables 94

Cross-Sectional OLS Regression Models:
3. Full Sample 97-98
4. Female Sample 109-110
5. Male Sample 111-112

Strength of Paired Correlation Z-Tests:
6. Depressed Mood 130
7. Self-Esteem 131

Longitudinal OLS Regression Models:
8. OLS Longitudinal Analyses Regressing Time 1 Variables on Time 2 Adolescent Depressed Mood and Self-Esteem 135-136

LIST OF FIGURES AND GRAPHS

Figure	Page
1. Children Residing with Married Mothers and Fathers, U.S. 1996.	16
2. Annual Adolescent Suicide Rates by Sex, U.S. 1996-2004	21
3. Female Adolescent Body Mass Index by Age	86
4. Male Adolescent Body Mass Index by Age	86
5. Path Diagram of Phase I Cross-Sectional Regression Models	88

INTRODUCTION

1.1. This book will examine the influences of dyadic parent-adolescent relationships on adolescent psychosocial well-being. Throughout the study I will explore parent-teen relationship quality, assessed through attachment and involvement, in order to investigate the ways in which children's relations with same-sex and cross-sex parents predict adolescent depressed mood. The current project will also investigate the processes by which adolescent self-esteem mediates familial relations and adolescent depressive symptomatology as well as examine the potential mediating effects of academic achievement as a precursor to self-esteem. By focusing on parent-child gender relations and gender-specific sources of teens' emotional outcomes, I will gauge the extent to which dyadic relationships influence male and female adolescents in distinct ways. Finally, longitudinal analyses will allow for developmental examination over time, thereby substantiating causation.

The complexity of adolescent self-concept formation and psychological well-being calls for meticulous attention to adolescents' relations with primary significant others and the critical role that gender plays in adolescent development. The present study seeks to offer a better understanding of how children's relationships with same-sex and cross-sex parents influence their well-being throughout the pivotal period in which teens form the final structure of their self-concepts and build emotional foundations needed to face the challenges of adolescence and ultimately adulthood. By further distinguishing domains of mothers' and fathers' relations with children, my analysis recognizes the unique contributions of different parental sources, namely relationship attachment and parental involvement. Findings that highlight the complexity of parent-adolescent gender dyads and adolescent developmental age will strengthen existing, more generalized parent-child social psychological research.

This book extends prior research of parent-child relationships and adolescent depressed mood in several distinct ways. First, I focus on the pervasive role that gender plays in influencing dyadic parent-adolescent relations and adolescent well-being by analyzing the specific ways in which mothers and fathers influence daughters' and sons' affective and cognitive outcomes. Second, I investigate the processes by which depressed mood may develop by determining the potential attenuating effects of both adolescent self-esteem and academic competency. Finally, the combination of cross-sectional and longitudinal methodology provides unique insight into the changes and enduring significance of dyadic parent-teen relations and other important variables on adolescent depressed mood and self-esteem over time.

1.2. Social psychologists have long asserted that humans are social beings who develop their own sense of selves based largely on people fundamental to their lives. Therefore, it is not surprising that many studies of adolescent depression have focused on parents, usually adolescents' primary figures or significant others (Demo et al. 1987; Freeman & Brown 2001; Metz 1995; Nada et al. 1992). Parents serve as principal role models for children's social learning and bestow optimism and love which are translated into children's subsequent hopefulness, self-worth, and own ability to love others (Bandura & Walters 1959; Ben-Zur 2003; Lansford et al. 2003). Children who feel securely attached to primary others develop healthy internal working models and self-understanding which promote social competency and resiliency (Black 2002; Kerns et al. 1996; Russell et al. 1998; Schneider & Atkinson 2001). A stable, secure, and supportive home environment provides a developing child with a dependable base for independence outside the home as well as a support base within the home in time of emotional need (Pappini & Roggman 1992).

Parents become salient resources for the enhancement of children's self-concepts via implicit and explicit appraisals. Cooley's looking glass self (1902), Mead's "taking the role of the other" (1934), and Sullivan's theory of interpersonal psychiatry (1953) represent classic symbolic interactionist theories of reflected appraisals, which contend that individuals define themselves through their perceptions of others' views of them. Positive appraisals protect, maintain, and enhance self-esteem as well as promote feelings of security, while negative appraisals damage self-esteem and engender anxiety. For teenagers experiencing heightened self-awareness and self-consciousness about how they are perceived by others, relations with parents become particularly significant (Baltes & Silverberg, 1994; DuBois et al., 1998; Harter, 1990).

Although the importance of the role parents play in children's developmental lives is irrefutable, literature remains conflicted as to which parent is most influential to children's emotional outcomes. Studies suggesting that children are more emotionally connected with, and thus more psychologically affected by, their mothers than their fathers (Chodorow 1974, 1978; Laible & Carlo 2004; Larson & Richards 1994) conflict with literature citing paternal influences as most significant to children's psychosocial functioning (Forehand & Nousiainen 1993; Gecas & Schwalbe 1986; Veneziano, 2000). The final assemblage of theories, which are associated with the present book's hypotheses, point to same-sex parent-child identification and relationships as most critical to children's development (Blos 1985; Crockenberg et al. 1996; Liu 2003; Maccoby 1994).

It is a primary goal of this book to focus on the critical role that gender and gender socialization play in shaping children's emotional outcomes. In doing so, I examine the differential influences of same-sex and cross-sex parents during the pivotal period in which adolescents form self-concepts and build secure emotional foundations. In order to promote healthy self-concept development research must better understand how each parent influences male and female adolescent self-esteem in distinct ways. Studies of children's psychosocial development must consistently account for socially constructed gender expectations that affect boys' and girls' behavior and values in profound and undeniable ways. Although it is impractical, though not impossible to transform deeply entrenched social structures, current research must seek to promote healthy adolescent development amid current gendered constructs.

The present manuscript recognizes that the relationship between the primary variables and adolescent depressed mood may not be direct, but rather may be mediated by other elements of a teenager's self-concept. My analyses examine whether, and to what extent, adolescent self-esteem mediates the processes that lead to depressed mood in order to disentangle the interrelated linkages of the primary self-concept measures. Identifying the specific role that self-esteem plays in the psychosocial processes by which dyadic parental relations may contribute to adolescent mood disturbance will be valuable to parents, psychologists, and educators concerned with the prevention and treatment of teen depression. By extending the analysis to assess the extent to which academic performance mediates the linkage between parent-teen relationship components and adolescent self-esteem, I aim to further disentangle the processes that lead to depressed mood. Although the journey through adolescence may be inevitably turbulent, the voyage through it can and should be eased with a clearer understanding of at-risk development. Research should seek to provide parents and educators with the insight needed to best prepare each individual child for the challenges of adolescence and ultimately adulthood.

This book aims to test five primary research objectives, listed as follows:

1. To examine the influence of dyadic parent-adolescent attachment and involvement on adolescent depressed mood.

2. To determine the extent to which self-esteem mediates the relationship between parent-adolescent relationship domains and adolescent depressed mood.

3. To assess the degree to which academic achievement mediates the relationship between parent-adolescent relationship domains and adolescent self-esteem.

4. To investigate the implications of gender on risks for adolescent depressed mood by analyzing boys' and girls' distinct evaluation and utilization of sources that impact scholastic performance, self-esteem, and mood disturbance.

5. To verify longitudinally the pathways of causation that lead to depressed mood in order to offer a developmental perspective of adolescent psychological health and influences thereof.

6. To assess longitudinally the stability or variability in respondents' psychosocial components of well-being and perceptions of relationship quality with parents over the course of one year.

1.3. Phase I presents a cross-sectional examination of the personal and structural sources of adolescent depressed mood, focusing on those pertaining to parent-adolescent relations. The impact of dyadic parent-teen relationship domains on children's depressed mood is first examined within the entire sample. Full sample analyses will then investigate and disentangle the extent to which adolescent academic achievement self-esteem act as mediators in the psychosocial processes that engender depressed mood. Supplemental regressions explore self-esteem and academic performance as dependent variables. The second part of Phase I separates the sample by gender, which offers critical insight into differential gender-specific sources of adolescent psychosocial outcomes. Seven male and seven female analyses mimic full sample regressions in structure. Finally, in order to examine the effects of adolescent gender and developmental age on the primary relationship, I integrate interaction regressions and strength of paired correlation z-test analyses.

Phase II incorporates a second wave of data for longitudinal regression analyses that examine the sources and trends of adolescent depressed mood over the course of a school year. I will investigate male and female samples separately for this phase of the study. The goal of the first set of longitudinal analyses is to consider the stability or variability in explanatory variables while analyzing their effects on teen depressed mood at time 2. I will then examine the causal processes that lead to self-esteem by inserting the latter self-esteem variable as the regression's outcome. Next, I will substitute time 2 mother-child and father-child attachment and involvement variables as individual dependent variables to observe each dyadic relationship's variability over time. All analyses control for respective time 1 variables. In total, Phase II includes a total of twelve ordinary least squares regressions analyses.

CHAPTER TWO
THEORETICAL FRAMEWORK

2.1. Theories of Parent-Adolescent Identification and Attachment

2.1.1. Contemporary Psychoanalysis

Although classic Freudian psychoanalytic theory is often considered outdated and even misogynistic, modern extrapolations have revitalized the aging, yet renowned theory. One such contemporary psychoanalytic theorist, Nancy Chodorow, focuses on the unconscious processes of infantile detachment and identification with mothers (Chodorow 1974, 1978). As maintained by neo-psychoanalytic theory, both boys and girls must eventually separate themselves from their primary caretakers in order to become autonomous beings. However, boys must further reject mothers and identify with fathers in their development of masculine selves. Accordingly, since it is the same-sex parent who becomes the important point of reference for healthy development of gender identity, a daughter is able to preserve her close and intimate connection with their initial source of identification in establishing her own identity. Sons, on the other hand, must emotionally detach themselves from their primary caretakers to seek out less available male figures.

Theory suggests that the tendency for females to grow up to define themselves in terms of their connections with others originates from primary feminine identification (Gilligan 1982). Due to prevailing filial-orientation, adolescent identity formation is especially challenging for girls for whom separation and individuation is not valued by society at large (Chodorow 1978). In contrast, Chodorow's same-sex identification lays the groundwork for males to define self-concepts in terms of independence and autonomy, which are socially valued traits, rather than closeness and intimacy.

Contemporary psychoanalytic theory is beneficial to examinations of dyadic parent-adolescent relationships. After all, if children do in fact internalize the behaviors and values of same-sex parents from infancy, those same-sex parents should become the primary role models by which youth not only learn gender-appropriate behavior and meaning, but perceive themselves as individuals.

2.1.2. *Parent-Child Attachment*

Influenced by Freudian psychoanalytic theory, John Bowlby became one of the leading scholars of attachment theory, which emphasizes the importance of close and supportive parent-child relationships to children's psychosocial development (Bowlby 1973, 1980). An infant's attachment to his or her mother is considered an instinctual and essential requirement of human life. Attachment theory revolves around the components of proximity, defined as the infant's or toddler's closeness to his or her caretaker, and security provided by a caretaker who acts as a safe base from which a child can explore his or her surrounding environment (Ainsworth et al. 1978; Noom et al. 1999; Sartor & Youniss 2002).

Attachment, usually representing child-mother emotional bonds, requires responsive and sensitive caregiving. According to attachment theory, children who feel securely attached to primary others develop healthy internal working models and self-understanding based on worthiness, which promote future social competency, independence, and resiliency (Black 2002; Kerns et al. 1996; Russell et al. 1998;

Schneider & Atkinson 2001; Stroufe 1983). Internal working models are continually developed and modified via interpersonal relations throughout life.

Parent-child attachment has been researched extensively in studies using Ainsworth's well-recognized "strange situation" experiment, which simply observed children's reactions when separated from mothers (Ainsworth et al. 1978). In Ainsworth's experiments, children were deemed as securely attached, insecurely attached and avoidant, insecurely attached and ambivalent-resistant, or insecurely attached and disoriented. Although a healthy, securely attached child tended to be upset when separated from his or her mother, the child was apt to be happy upon her return. These children freely investigated proximal surroundings and were able to engage socially with strangers when mothers were present. In contrast, insecure attachment domains corresponded to children who resisted exploration and were anxious or indifferent toward strangers, or even mothers. Furthermore, insecurely attached children became extremely agitated when separated from their mothers and were likely to display resentment toward them when reunited. Insecure attachment is theorized to evolve from either disengaged mothering or mothering that is engaged, but only in a way that suits the caretaker's personal interests. According to the theory, children who experience disoriented insecure attachment are unable to cope with social situations. These children are often frightened by their caretakers or internalize their caretaker's distress.

Although attachment theory originally focused on secure bonds shared by mothers and their infants, the prominent theory has since evolved to address older youth, adolescent, and even adult attachment with parents or significant others. Emphasized are the importance of warm, connected, and supportive mothers and fathers in instilling positive self-image and providing a secure base from which teenagers, for instance, can effectively explore the world apart from their parents (Bretherton 1994; Freeman & Brown 2001; O'Koon 1997). The theory is particularly suitable for studies of adolescence since this life course stage exemplifies an unprecedented period of evolving emotions and psychosocial development. In fact, insecure attachment has been found to predispose adolescents to emotional disorders as well as self-inflicted anger (Taylor et al. 1997; Zimmerman 1999) while secure attachment has been reported to correspond with psychological resiliency, anger control management, and positive relationships with others (Mikulincer 1998).

2.2. Social Cognitive Theory

Stemming from social learning theory, Albert Bandura proposed a social cognitive theory that focused on self-beliefs of individuals, who he viewed as active and self-reflective participants in their environments (Bandura 1986). Bandura, who repeatedly clarified that "people are producers as well as products of social systems" (Bandura 2001, pp. 1), saw a triadic reciprocality, or dynamic interplay, between individual personality, behavior, and environment. As an example, children of parents who provide love and support and portray positive representations of social beings learn behavioral skills via authoritative discipline, positive appraisals, and vicarious learning. Consequently, as these children mature they are more likely than children lacking positive significant others to hold positive self-beliefs and cognitions (personality); to develop healthy social networks and become productive, law-abiding individuals (behavior); and become active and influential agents in society (environment). However, the emphasis on personal agency purports that familial factors, such as quality of parenting or familial economic conditions, do not directly predict children's behavior. Instead, according to Bandura, familial factors influence children's self-esteem, aspirations, self-control, and other emotions that are so critical to behavioral self-regulatory capabilities and outcomes. Throughout this book I will reject an overly passive view of child development in favor of social cognitive perspectives that recognize the power of human agency and self-creativity. Nevertheless, it is important to note that within this framework parental influence is acknowledged as the critical component of children's psychosocial development.

Social-cognitive theory is especially relevant to this study because adolescence marks the period in which teens develop autonomous identities and mastery over social skills in preparation for adulthood. Healthy development during adolescence fosters human agency needed to solve problems cognitively, guide and regulate personal actions, and make judgments regarding one's own behavior and self. Social-cognitive theory hinges on the concept of self-efficacy, or individuals' beliefs regarding their "capabilities to organize and execute courses of action required to attain designated types of performances" (Bandura 1986, pp. 391). In his analysis of human behavior Bandura maintained that humans must be confident in their abilities in order to possess incentive to strive for, and thus accomplish, specified goals. In effect, self-efficacy works in a self-perpetuating manner in which high self-efficacy leads to successful behavior which, in turn, boosts one's self-confidence. On the other hand, a person with low self-efficacy is likely to fail to reach (or even attempt) goals, which only further denigrates his or her sense of self-efficacy.

According to social cognitive theory, proactive and agentic beings exercise much control over their psychological states, personal behavior, and social relationships. Not surprisingly, emotional well-being is related to self-efficacy. Reducing negative emotion and increasing self-esteem can elevate one's self-efficacy while enhanced self-efficacy positively affects one's psychological sense of self.

2.2.1. *The Relationship between Self-Efficacy and Self-Esteem*

While self-efficacy is defined as one's self-confidence to succeed at a domain-specific task, self-esteem is the overall evaluation of oneself. For example, an individual's self-efficacy beliefs in regard to academics may be extremely high while his or her athletic self-efficacy may be extremely low. In contrast, global self-esteem embodies one's sense of self and cannot be partitioned into separate domains. Social self-efficacy, representing an individual's confidence in his or her abilities to socially interact with others, is one of the most critical realms in which self-efficacy operates and is also the dimension most closely related to self-esteem.

While many studies have used measures of self-efficacy and self-esteem to assess adolescent well-being, very few have attempted to use the similar psychosocial concepts within a single analysis. Still, regardless of whether self-efficacy or self-esteem has represented the central variable, the majority of research outcomes have been strikingly similar. Like self-esteem, adolescent self-efficacy has been linked to supportive parents and peers, delinquency, academic achievement, and depressed mood (Bandura et al. 1999; McFarlane et al. 1995). Moreover, studies of self-efficacy in youth have found that girls' emotional well-being is more dependent on perceived social competence than boys' emotional well-being (Bandura et al. 1999). While a plethora of studies have demonstrated significant correlation between self-esteem and self-efficacy (Betz & Klein 1996; Wulff & Steitz 1999), longitudinal analyses have unearthed causation effects in which self-esteem predicted social competence (Crocker & Luhtanen 2003). Nevertheless, inconsistent research has led most researchers to resolve that the two measures are too similar to be considered statistically different in academic research (Stanley & Murphy 1997). It is for this reason that the current manuscript focuses on the concept of self-esteem and does not attempt to incorporate self-efficacy measures into the analysis. However, considering the import of self-efficacy to certain variables, it will be acknowledged throughout this book when pertinent.

2.3. Social Capital Theory

In 1988, James Coleman coined the theory of social capital by merging theories of socialization and neoclassical economic concepts of rational action. The premise of social capital theory, an extension of financial, physical, and human capital models, rests on an actor's social relations with others, which are used as resources to gain human capital and pursue goals. While the theory extends to all social connections, those between parents and children and the subsequent outcomes for children's social and cognitive well-being applies most centrally to this manuscript. Accordingly, caring and attentive parents provide social capital to their children while uncaring and uninvolved parents deprive their children of the resources so important to behavioral and cognitive success. In effect, the social investments parents bestow upon their children should result in their children's attainment of personal capital.

Coleman specifies the following forms of social capital: expectations, information channels, and social norms (Coleman 1988). The first category is fulfilled when high quality parent-child relations based on mutual trust enable parents' explicit and implicit expectations to be both desired and fulfilled by children. Because children trust their parents, they feel obligated and personally aspire to successfully meet those expectations (e.g. striving for high grades, choice of friends, staying out of trouble). Next, information channels provide communicable information useful for positive outcomes. For example, parents who have positive sense of selves or received high marks in school themselves may have insight and advice for their own children. Finally, social norms are transferred from parents to children throughout childhood. Children from stable homes learn and internalize social norms and values that foster their development as honest and socially competent individuals. For instance, warm and supportive parents likely instill in children the need to share with playmates or behave gender appropriately.

2.3.1. Familial Resources of Social Capital

Parents provide children with a variety of financial, human, and social capital to help them through the adolescent years. Financial capital, in the form of parental income, affords physical resources; human capital, such as parental educational attainment or parental upbringing, supplies and encourages a particular intellectual and social learning environment; and social capital, as just discussed, is based on parent-child relations and provides resources for children's social, behavioral, and identity development. Notably, Coleman contends that parents' human capital "may be irrelevant to outcomes for children if parents are not an important part of their children's lives (pp. S110)". That is to say that even if a parent possesses a plethora of human capital, a child's acquisition of such capital will not be achieved if communication between the parent and child is deficient or if the parent is not involved in his or her son's or daughter's life.

In order to examine familial social capital in pragmatic terms, it is essential to recognize the reality of American family life, in which only a fraction of families consist of a three-person mother-father-child household. Whereas 77% of children ages 0-17 resided with two married parents in 1980, estimates decreased to 67% by 2006 (U.S. Census Bureau 2006). Figure 1 illustrates the demographic residential composition of U.S. teens in 1996, a year in which the current sample of respondents would have been teenagers.

Figure 1. Children residing with married mothers and fathers, U.S. 1996

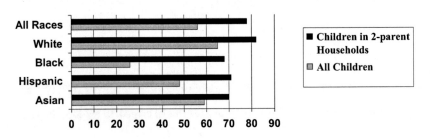

Source: U.S. Census Bureau, *Survey of Families and Households*, 1996.

Moreover, the U.S. Census Bureau estimated that only 21.4% of children resided in homes in which they were only children in 1996. Familial social capital extends to all members of the household and considers how each member influences the allotment of social capital resources to children. Coleman contends that single-parent headed households, dual-working parent households, and siblings all work to diminish the resources available to residential children. For instance, divorce is believed to halve the physical presence of parental figures in the household while the occupational demands forced on an employed mother are thought to minimize her accessibility to her children (Coleman 1988). According to social capital theory, the presence of siblings dilutes the attention each child receives from parents. Given that the present analysis is comprised of children residing with two biological parents only, the effect of single-parent homes is not investigated. However, number of siblings and maternal occupational status are both incorporated in the analyses.

2.4. Theoretical Framework

Throughout this book, I will integrate theories of psychoanalytic identification, attachment, social cognition, and social capital to frame my investigation of parent-child relations and adolescent emotional and cognitive well-being. Considering the complexity of the mediating and outcome variables, theories will be interpreted according to the respective focal variable at issue. Furthermore, given the intersecting nature of the theories, the theoretical discussion is blended when suitable.

CHAPTER THREE
BACKGROUND & HYPOTHESES

3.1. Adolescent Identity Formation

Adolescence has long been considered a pivotal period in human development. It is during adolescence that an individual embarks upon an unprecedented journey of self-exploration and gains a sense of personal autonomy and responsibility beyond parents. As the metaphorical bridge connecting childhood and adulthood, adolescence becomes vital to life course trajectories and future psychosocial success and well-being. It is during the years of twelve and nineteen that children undergo the significant psychosocial developmental period in which they begin to define themselves as autonomous individuals and confront roles of adulthood (Erikson 1968; Rosenberg 1986). As early as a century ago G. Stanley Hall referred to adolescence as "the birthday of the imagination" (1904, vol.1:313) since children first recognize themselves as distinct individuals. Increased autonomy, personal responsibility, and developing self-definitions can nevertheless be emotionally challenging for maturing teenagers.

Developmentalists have universally reported that the most intense psychosocial disturbance transpires between the ages of 12 and 14, otherwise known as early adolescence (Rosenberg et al. 1973). It is during this first stage of adolescence that a child first encounters pressure to detach from parental figures and the security they offer in order to develop a sense of oneself as an individual entity. By mid-adolescence, or roughly 15 to 17 years of age, self-exploration continues and teenagers are thought to begin to discover who they truly are and how they fit into their surrounding world.

Finally, self-concepts are thought to begin to solidify by late adolescence, or 18 to 19 years of age. Although Erikson's 1968 theory of adolescent identity formation has, for the most part, withstood the rigors of decades of adolescent research, his developmental framework has been challenged. Most scholars now believe that identity development is a much slower process than previously thought. In fact, new developments in identity research have prompted scholars to introduce a new stage of "emerging adulthood", which links adolescence and young adulthood, and is characterized by residential instability and continued identity exploration (Arnett 2000). Although this book focuses on teenagers, it is important to recognize that psychosocial development does not cease at the end of adolescence, but rather continues well beyond the teen years.

All in all, despite considerable research, the timetable in which adolescent identities are fully formed remains unclear. What is clear, however, is that teenagers actively evaluate themselves as individual entities and increasingly solidify and organize self-concepts. This book focuses on psychosocial dynamics of adolescents' selves that indisputably undergo massive psychosocial transformation throughout the period.

3.2. Adolescent Depressed Mood

While the journey through adolescence is relatively stable for most individuals, others face dangerous and sometimes fatal outcomes. Those adolescents who do suffer significant psychosocial impairment are often left with psychological "scars" that adversely affect their life satisfaction, social functioning, and emotional health well into adulthood. Ironically, the majority of past adolescent research has focused on adolescents' externalizing problems (e.g. delinquency, dropping out of school), even though internalized problems (e.g. low self-esteem, depression) are much more likely to persist beyond adolescence. The following section, which examines literature of adolescent depressive symptomatology, frames what is known regarding the sources, development, and consequences of teen depression.

3.2.1. Short-term Risks

Depressed mood is characterized by heightened negative cognition towards oneself and his or her surroundings. Though difficult to quantify, experts believe that 10-15% of adolescents suffer from depressive symptoms (Smucker et al. 1986) which include hopelessness, despair, apathy, excessive pessimism, guilt, and exaggerated responsibility for negative events. Depressed mood during adolescence was once considered a natural and normal aspect of the challenging developmental period. In fact, preeminent psychoanalyst Anna Freud famously stated that "to be normal during the adolescent period is by itself abnormal (1958)". However, contrary to such historic accounts, researchers now recognize that adolescent depressed mood can transcend into the dangerous and alarming epidemic of depression (Call et al. 2002).

Though often used interchangeably, depression, unlike depressed mood, is defined as experiencing five or more stated symptoms of mood disturbance for at least two weeks (Center for Mental Health Services 1998; Smucker et al. 1986). Please refer to Appendix A for the National Institute of Mental Health's official listing of depressive symptoms. Empirical evidence suggests that 5 to 8 percent of teens have depression at any given time and that one in five teens will suffer from depression before they reach adulthood (Son & Kirchner 2000; University of Michigan Depression Center 2006).

However, figures likely misrepresent the true risks given that depression is vastly under diagnosed in adolescent populations.

Such prolonged negative affect is associated with suppressed cognition as well as interpersonal impairment. For example, depressed adolescents are susceptible to drug and alcohol abuse, poor social functioning, school dropouts, and even suicide (Diego et al. 2003). Experts estimate that one in five teens have legitimate suicidal thoughts, otherwise known as suicide ideation (Grunbaum et al. 2001). Youth suicides, which have tripled since 1970 (New York Times 2004), are now the third leading cause of adolescent death (Anderson 2002). Adolescents with major depression are twelve times more likely than non-depressed adolescents to commit suicide (National Institute of Mental Health 2000). Statistics also depict gender discrepancies in which 15 to 19 year old boys are four to five times more likely to commit suicide than their female counterparts even though girls are twice as likely to attempt suicide (Centers for Disease Control and Prevention 1999; Gould et al. 2003). Figure 2 illustrates national suicide rates for male and female teens.

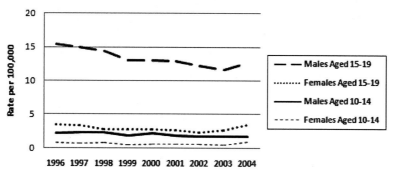

Figure 2. Annual U.S. suicide rates for male and female adolescents, 1996-2004

Source: *National Vital Statistics System*, United States, 2004.

Research estimates that, on average, suicide ideation rates increase throughout early adolescence, peak during mid-adolescence, and diminish in late adolescence and beyond (Carlson & Cantwell 1982; Kosky et al. 1986; Lewinsohn et al. 1996). However, the fact that the highest suicide completion rates occur between 20 to 24 years of age indicates that the progression from inception of depressive symptomatology to suicidal tendencies is somewhat prolonged. Although disturbing, the many stages that seem to precede actual suicide attempts suggest that suicide is also quite preventable.

3.2.2. *Long-term Risks*

Unfortunately teenage depression is not restricted to the years of adolescence. According to a 2003 US Surgeon General report, the majority of adolescent depression persists or reemerges in adulthood. Researchers estimate that adolescent depressive disorders double or quadruple risks for adulthood depression (Pine et al. 1999). In general, depressive symptomatology in children does not begin to increase significantly until early adolescence, at which point it is estimated to increase slightly throughout the developmental period and into adulthood (Avenevoli & Steinberg 2001). In a recent longitudinal survey, Dr. Lewinsohn and colleagues revealed that respondents who suffered even a single episode of major depression during adolescence were significantly more likely to exhibit extreme psychopathology as adults (Lewinsohn et al. 2003). Depressed mood in adolescence is linked to adult impairments such as chronic pessimism, career failure, deficient interpersonal relationships, substance abuse, and life dissatisfaction. Predictions that depression will be the second leading cause of disease and disability by 2020 emphasize the need to better understand its risk factors for adolescents, the age range in which depression is believed to arise (World Health Organization 1999; Sorenson et al. 1991).

3.2.3. *Origins of Depressed Mood*

Epidemiological research confirms that genetic predisposition can facilitate depression. However, with the exception of manic-depressive (bi-polar) disorder, which is actually quite rare among adolescents, the most common risk factors are thought to be environmental. Two well-known facilitators of depressed mood include stressful life events and poor psychological coping capacity (Nolen-Hoeksema et al. 1991). Lack of involvement, support, and warmth from parents, family discord or divorce, abuse or neglect, loss of a loved one, demise of an intimate relationship, and numerous other traumatic events can precipitate depressed mood (Brent et al.1994; Pfeffer 1994). While stressful life events and lack of resiliency, or the ability to rebound from hardship, undoubtedly put individuals at increased risk for depressed mood, I believe a more all-encompassing source to consider lies with children's parents. After all, parents not only have the capacity to mitigate stressful life events, but upbringing builds children's character and self-esteem to manage and overcome stress that will inevitably emerge in life. As stated, a myriad of factors can instigate depression and this book does not suggest that parents have the power to insulate children from depressive risks altogether. Instead, I contend that parental support plays an important role in protecting children from depression. The primary goal of this analysis is to dissect sources of adolescent depressed mood that stem from those relationships considered most fundamental and vital to child development, namely children's relations with parents.

3.3. Parent-Adolescent Relationships and Adolescent Depressed Mood

Just as parents can be powerful engines in facilitating children's well-being, unloving and unsupportive parental figures can have a devastating impact of children's psychological health. For example, households in which parents are not readily available for children in times of emotional need or fail to show affection toward children are found to adversely affect children's future interpersonal relationships and psychosocial development. The enormous influence that parents have on children's mental dispositions can be examined in a number of different ways.

As previously mentioned, attachment theory emphasizes the importance of close and supportive parent-child relationships to children's psychosocial development (Ainsworth et al. 1978; Bowlby 1958, 1982; Noom et al. 1999; Sartor & Youniss 2002). Warm, connected, and engaged parent-child attachment is essential in instilling positive self-image and providing a secure base from which children can fruitfully explore their surroundings (Bretherton 1994; Frank et al. 1990; Freeman & Brown 2001; O'Koon 1997). In effect, healthy attachment relations cultivate competent internal working models and self-understanding which promote social functioning, independence, and resiliency (Black 2002; Kerns et al. 1996; Russell et al. 1998; Schneider & Atkinson 2001).

Empirical evidence suggests that adolescents whose parents fail to show affection are more likely to be depressed than peers (Rey 1995) while warm and sympathetic parents decrease the likelihood that children will become depressed (MacFarlane at al. 1995). Armsden and colleagues (1990) compared samples of adolescents with clinical depression, resolved depression, and no depressive affect to conclude that depressed respondents perceived significantly lower levels of parental attachment than the other samples of adolescents. Overall, a consensus among researchers maintains significant association between low attachment to parents and depressed youth (Essau 2004; Nada Raja et al. 1992).

Social cognitive theory illustrates the conscious and unconscious influences that parents have on children's subsequent personality and behavior. For instance, findings that adolescents with parents who have negative dispositions are more depressed underscore the significance of modeling behavior (Pike & Plomin 1996). Authoritative parenting, characterized by high expectations and high responsiveness, conveys clear and structured behavioral expectations to children within a supportive environment. The cognitive benefits of authoritative upbringing are found to engender self-regulated and cooperative children, which also fosters children's cognitive, social, and psychological competency. Involved parents are found to have greater awareness of stressors in adolescents' lives, which enable parents to act in such ways that buffer negative implications (Hartos & Power 2000). Clear evidence suggests that adolescents whose parents are not responsive or who are unengaged tend to be more depressed than those whose parents are responsive, communicative, and supportive (Gould et al. 1996; Maccoby & Martin 1986; Radziszewska et al. 1996).

In addition, relationships between parents and children provide resources to children in the form of social capital. Parental measures of mastery and happiness, healthy home environments, parent-child communication, realistic parental expectations, and parental involvement have all been found to ward off behavioral problems and negative emotion in children (Lasko & Field 1996; Parcel & Menaghan 1993).

Depressed adolescents are more likely to have parents who are less supportive and less involved than non-depressed adolescents (Hoffman & Su 1998).

When children confront newfound pressures to become more autonomous and independent during adolescence, their relationships with their parents inevitably evolve. Developmental and early psychoanalytic theorists have historically viewed adolescence as a period of individuation in which children rebel against parents in their search for autonomy (Rubin 1984). Aristotle once wrote that adolescents were "heated by Nature as drunken men by wine" (Arnett 1999, 317). Most contemporary literature, however, no longer views parent-adolescent relationships as embittered with turmoil, but rather recognizes relationships in which, despite increased conflict, most adolescents remain close to and continue to identify with parents throughout the period (Gecas & Seff 1990; Guerney & Arthur 1984; Ogletree et al. 2002; Walker & Greene 1986). In fact, in a study of 650 adolescents, Steinberg and colleagues (2001) found that three out of four adolescents felt close to their parents and less than ten percent experienced deterioration in their relationships during the period. Likewise, Ogletree, Jone, and Coyl (2002) found that both fathers' and sons' perceptions of father-son companionship, sustained contact, and support did not change significantly across the adolescent developmental period.

As it turns out, classic notions of adolescence as a time of intense parent-child conflict are considered to be greatly exaggerated. This is unfortunate considering that research findings corroborate the contention that teens' healthy development of autonomous selves is best achieved within a context of close and supportive relations with parents.

Despite the significance of gender in dyadic parent-child relationships, research often neglects the complexity of parent-child interactions by merging mothers and fathers into a single parental variable or representing the parental variable through only one parent's perspective, most commonly the mother. I consider conjugal representations of parental influence to be immensely deficient. In order to promote healthy psychosocial development research must better understand how and to what extent each parent affects adolescent depression in distinct ways. The present investigation examines adolescent relations with both mothers and fathers through adolescent perceptions of parental caring, parental warmth, relationship closeness, and parental involvement.

Clearly, both parental attachment and involvement facilitate positive outcomes in children. However, given the significance of parental warmth, caring, and closeness to children's self-understandings, the parental attachment dimension of parent-child relations is expected to be more influential to children's internal emotions than parental involvement. I argue that attachment to parents is intimately tied to children's psychological and expressive outcomes, particularly during the challenging period of adolescence. Through secure attachment relations with significant others, adolescents develop healthy internal working models and competent self-understanding that insulate them from psychological dangers and foster health minds.

3.3.1. *Phase I, Hypothesis 1*

H1. Although each parent-adolescent relationship domain should be inversely associated with adolescent depressed mood, parent-adolescent attachment should be a stronger buffer against depressed mood than parental involvement.

3.4. Gender-Specific Sources of Adolescent Depressed Mood

Gender has profound effects on adolescent psychological distress. Not only are adolescent girls more susceptible to depressive affect, but depression is manifested in gender-specific ways (Avison & McAlpine 1992; Gore et al. 1992; Nolen-Hoeksema 1987; Nolen-Hoeksema & Girgus 1994). The present analysis stresses the differential impact of gender on adolescent male and female psychological health and well-being.

Although there are no known gender differences in rates of depression among preadolescents (Keenan & Hipwell 2005), adolescent females are twice as likely to become depressed as adolescent males (Angold et al. 1999; Nolen-Hoeksema & Girgus 1994). In fact, in a recent longitudinal study of 1,322 teenagers, researchers found that an astounding 24% of 16 to 19 year old females suffered from at least one episode of major depression as compared to 10% of males (Galambos 2004). Clearly, adolescent depression is an alarming problem for both boys and girls, but significantly higher rates of depression among female teens must be deciphered in order to better comprehend the disproportionate short and long term risks.

The National Mental Health Association contends that the gender discrepancy in adulthood depression, in which depression is also twice as common in females as males, initiates during adolescence. In corroboration of NMHA findings, Kessler and colleagues (1993) reported a lack of gender differences found in adult-onset depression. The researchers explained adult women's higher depression rates entirely by gender differences in depression beginning in adolescence. However, conflicting research suggests that the gender gap in depression does widen throughout adulthood in response to pervasive cultural gender inequity (Mirowsky 1996; Sprock & Yoder 1997).

Mirowsky (1996) contends that adulthood gender stratification and unequal role statuses give rise to expanding gender differences in depression with age. In contrast to the discordant beliefs regarding gender's bearing on lifespan depression, the gender disparity in adolescent depression is irrefutable. The present analysis will focus on the adolescent time period in an attempt to unravel the sociological reasons for girls' greater predisposition to depressive symptomatology.

Extensive literature concurs that girls tend to suffer considerably more emotional distress prior to, and during adolescence than their male counterparts (Avison & McAlpine 1992; Gjerde et al. 1988; Kling et al. 1999; Nolen-Hoeksema & Girgus 1994). Boys are believed to feel more confident and masterful than girls when they leave their home environments to encounter the challenges of adolescence (Quatman & Watson 2001). Specialists most often cite female orientation toward social relationships as the primary gender-specific precursor to depressed mood. Heightened interpersonal stressors during adolescence make teenage girls especially vulnerable to emotional impairment. To study adolescent boys and girls as if they embody the same emotional and behavioral characteristics and are at equal risk for depression neglects the extensive impact of societal gender beliefs.

A broader recognition of how patriarchal society, which deems women inferior to men, impacts children's socialization is necessary to thoroughly understand the massive gender disparity in adolescent male and female depression. According to feminine scholars, when young girls look toward same-sex significant others as role models, most witness mothers, whether employed or not, who manage domestic duties and defer responsibility to husbands, who typically hold dominant positions in the household.

Moreover, youth recognize that men maintain the most powerful and lucrative positions in society and, according to concepts of gender status beliefs, are generally deemed to be more intelligent, competent, and independent than women (Ridgeway 1997). Feminist theory condemns patriarchal social structures that depict and expect women to be dependent, passive, and amenable while men are pressured to be unemotional and authoritative. In effect, girls and boys are believed to internalize societal gender status beliefs of femininity and masculinity in their attempts to attain socially appropriate identities.

Childhood socialization that stresses compliance with gender role expectations has extraordinary influence over boys' and girls' formed behavior and dispositional traits (Beutel & Marini 1995; Renk 2003). Entrenched social guidelines "masculinize" boys and "feminize" girls according to gender ideals of appropriate behavior and expectations (Kohlberg 1966; Marini 1990). Throughout childhood girls are socialized to value relationships and connectedness while boys are taught to be more individualistic and independent (Beutel & Marini 1995; Fischer et al. 1989). Through life-long processes of social interaction, learning gender prescriptions, and "doing gender" boys and girls ascertain gender appropriate behavior and acquire personalities that distinguish them from the opposite sex (West & Zimmerman 1991). For example, Nielson deemed that females were better than men at "intimate, self-disclosing, emotional communication because they have been taught and have been rehearsing these skills since early childhood (2001, 5)". As a result of gender socialization females tend to internalize traits that are more expressive and communal than males while males are apt to be more agentic and competitive than females (Beutel & Marini 1995).

Due to children's embodiment of different gender prescriptions, boys and girls are likely to hold dissimilar views of what they consider to be relevant and central to their self-concepts and what they feel is unimportant or peripheral. For example, close and intimate relationships tend to be more salient to the relationship-oriented self-definitions of females than independently self-defined males (Kohlberg 1966). In her study of Japanese culture, Dorinne Kondo stated that relations-focused individuals consider themselves a "single thread in a richly textured fabric of relationships (1990, 33)". The analogy depicts female identities as enmeshed in many relationships, whether positive or negative. Such embeddedness results in interpersonal connections that are deeply tied to female sense of selves.

Clearly, the factors that influence adolescent psychosocial well-being are not found in a set of generalized components, but are very specific to each individual (Rosenberg 1979). Rosenberg's concept of psychological centrality recognizes that, "the impact of any given component on global self-esteem will depend on its importance or unimportance, centrality or peripherality, in the individual's cognitive structure (Rosenberg & Pearlin 1978, 67)". Since interpersonal relationships are only as influential as they are salient to an individual's self-definition, relationships are expected to be more significant to the psychological states of girls than boys.

Examination of socialized gender-specific dispositions is important to understanding the manifestation of depression in boys and girls. Since girls are raised to be more expressive and emotional than boys, it is reasonable to assume that girls deal with frustration and hardship internally rather than externally. In contrast, parents and society teach boys to suppress emotions in order to embody instrumental masculinity. As a result, boys who experience comparable stressors should be inclined to express themselves externally or behaviorally, rather than internally or emotionally. Accordingly, troubled girls should be predisposed to mental psychopathology, such as depression, while boys should be prone to antisocial behavior, such as violence, delinquency, or drug abuse.

Unless research becomes more focused on the critical role of gender and gender socialization in shaping emotional temperament, girls who embark upon adolescence less prepared than their male counterparts will continue to suffer emotional disadvantages throughout their lives. To study boys and girls as if they embody the same emotional and behavioral characteristics and are at equal risk for depression neglects the extensive impact of societal gender constructs.

3.4.1. *Parent-Child Gender Dyads*

As discussed previously, the few child development studies that have accounted for both parent and adolescent gender have produced conflicting results. While some suggest that children identify more strongly with their same-sex parent (Blos 1985; Liu 2003; Maccoby 1994), other literature contends that both boys and girls are more impacted by their relations with mothers than fathers (Laible & Carlo, 2004; Larson & Richards 1994; Paterson et al. 1994; Thornton et al. 1995) or vice versa (Forehand & Nousiainen, 1993; Veneziano, 2000). The fact that literature examining the independent effects of maternal and paternal attachment and involvement has revealed significant differences in adolescents' cognitive and emotional outcomes illustrates the importance of comprehensive dyadic investigations.

Demographic and cultural shifts have also changed the roles of mothers and fathers in contemporary families. Domestic mothers and breadwinning fathers of the 1950's have transformed drastically. Today, only one-quarter of American children reside in homes in which fathers are sole wage earners and two-thirds of preschoolers have working mothers (Cabrera et al. 2000). While mothers are still primarily responsible for domestic and childcare duties, they are no longer culturally confined to homes or stigmatized for having careers outside the home. In addition, fatherhood has evolved into a more involved, co-parenting role over the past few centuries. Cabrera and colleagues (2000) reported that fathers spent an average of 30-45% as much time with children as mothers did three decades ago, but by 2000 spent an estimated 67% as much time with children as mothers did during the week and 87% as much time on weekends. The modernization of gendered division of labor has altered parent-child relationships and will continue to do so well into the future. Clearly, mothers and fathers experience disparate relations with sons and daughters that will continue to impact boys' and girls' emotional and cognitive well-being in unique and evolving ways.

Although most scholars believe that parents retain relatively stable relationships with children during adolescence, it is probable that heightened gender pressures accompanying the developmental period alter the interpersonal dynamics between children and their parents. Psychoanalytic theories posit that, despite increased detachment, same-sex parents become the most important points of reference for children coping with how best to comply with their respective gender. Such theories focus on children's innate need to identify with and internalize respective masculine or feminine traits of same-sex parents for healthy psychosocial development (Freud 1949; Parsons

1964). During the critical developmental phase of adolescence gender becomes the primary identity by which adolescents can clearly define and distinguish themselves from others. Hill & Lynch (1983) refer to this as a time of "gender-role intensification" in which gender reaches unprecedented salience and boys and girls become most sex-differentiated (Eme 1984; Garmezy & Rutter 1983). When confronted with unprecedented social and personal pressure to fulfill appropriate gender identity definitions, adolescents look toward same-sex role models, namely parents, for support and guidance. This project argues that as gender becomes exceedingly salient upon the transition to adolescence, so should the relationship a child shares with his or her same-sex parent. Given the psychological importance placed on children's relations with same-sex parents, attachment to same-sex parents should be more predicative of adolescent psychological state than attachment to cross-sex parents.

3.4.2. Phase I, Hypotheses 2 and 3

H2. Same-sex parent-adolescent relationship domains are expected to be stronger predictors of adolescent depressed mood than cross-sex parent-adolescent relationship domains.

H3. Adolescent female depressed mood should be more dependent on relationships with both cross-sex and same-sex parents than adolescent male depressed mood.

3.5. Mediation of Self-Esteem

It is important to consider that the relationship between the stated risk factors and adolescent depressed mood may not be direct, but may actually be mediated by other elements of an adolescent's self-concept. The following section will examine whether, and to what extent, self-esteem impacts the processes that lead to depressed mood.

Self-esteem, or one's self-evaluation and feelings of personal worth, is a fundamental component of identity formation and adolescent development (Simmons & Rosenberg 1975). Social psychologists assert that humans are inherently motivated to define themselves favorably in relation to others. Positive self-views, in which desired self-definitions are achieved enhance self-esteem while failure to meet desired selves lowers self-esteem. In Morris Rosenberg's comprehensive analysis of self-concept formation, he explains that a person with high self-esteem feels worthy as a human being while a person with low self-esteem "lacks respect for himself, considers himself unworthy, inadequate, or otherwise seriously deficient as a person" (Rosenberg 1979, 54).

Undoubtedly, one's sense of self is critical to developmental trajectories and future well-being (Baumeister et al. 2003; Clausen 1991; Erikson 1968; Marcia 1993). While positive self-esteem is correlated with interpersonal competence and life satisfaction (DuBois et al. 1998; Hansford & Hattie 1982; Liu et al. 1992), adolescents with low self-esteem are found to be susceptible to harmful outcomes such as unhappiness, loneliness, and eating disorders (Chubb 1997; Harter 1998; Owens 1994; Pipher 1994). In the present section, I focus on the established connection between depleted self-esteem and mood disturbance.

Self-esteem serves an important role as a coping mechanism that buffers against negative challenges and stresses (Kling et al. 1999; Roberts & Bengtson 1993). The buffer hypothesis highlights the self-perpetuating nature of self-esteem in which individuals with positive self-esteem are emotionally equipped to fend off threats to their self-concept while individuals with low self-esteem are more vulnerable to such threats which, in turn, further denigrate their sense of selves (Burke 1996; Cast & Burke 2002). There is no doubt that self-esteem plays a critical role in adolescent psychosocial development and, therefore, research must clearly identify the sources that both cultivate and diminish it.

Overall, self-esteem is thought to remain relatively stable over the course of adolescence. For the most part, research agrees that early adolescence signifies the period in which youth have the lowest self-esteem and hold the most negative self-perceptions (Eccles et al. 1989). Although self-esteem suffers instability upon the transition to adolescence, it is thought to increase slightly throughout the period (Alasker & Olweus 1992; Harter 1998). Simmons and Rosenberg (1973) maintain that self-esteem surges at roughly sixteen years of age. Nevertheless, the developmental trajectory of adolescent self-esteem is still widely disputed.

While most adolescents' sense of selves persevere during the challenging period, other adolescents suffer serious damage to psychological well-being (Deihl et al. 1997). Gender, in particular, has pronounced impact on the mental constitution of self-esteem. For example, girls tend to have lower self-esteem than boys at all ages (Kling et al. 1999; Quatman & Watson 2001). Also not surprising, such self-esteem differentials are found to be most extreme during early adolescence. Feminist studies point to adolescent girls' identification with female identities, which are deemed to be inferior to male identities in society at large, as suppressive and damaging to girls' sense of selves (Bohan 1973; Deaux 1984; Thorne 1997). Although societal gender status beliefs undoubtedly play a role in the development of adolescent self-esteem, there is much more at work. Investigating the sources of self-esteem as well as the processes by which self-esteem forms will shed light on females' propensity for lower self-esteem.

3.5.1. Self-Esteem and Depression

Clearly, self-esteem and depressed mood are associated. An overwhelming body of research that has explored the association between the psychological concepts has estimated varying levels of correlation, in which high self-esteem is linked to healthy psychological functioning and low self-esteem is related to depressed mood (Ouellet & Joshi 1986, r= -.28; Smith & Betz 2002, r= -.66). Although the association between self-esteem and depression is well-established, academics still wrestle over the direction of that relationship. Some social psychologists contend that self-esteem and depression maintain a bi-directional causal relationship in which the negative emotions of the psychological states feed off of each other (Rosenberg et al. 1989). Still, the most rigorous and conclusive research findings suggest that the failure to fulfill the fundamental human motive for positive self-esteem does in fact precede and predict depressed mood (Beck 1967; Owens 1994)

While acknowledging that depressed mood can eventually work to deplete levels of self-esteem, the strongest evidence points to self-esteem as antecedent to depressed mood. Aaron Beck's well-recognized cognitive model of depression (1967) theorizes that negative self-views are the key causal component of depressed mood. Several recent studies have added support to Beck's theory. For example, Brown & Harris (1978) posited that children deprived of parents, either literally or emotionally, suffer negative self-esteem and self-worth which, in turn, lead to depression. Wilkinson (2004) implemented structural equation modeling to analyze three studies, each using different samples of teenagers, in order to investigate the relationship between parental attachment, peer attachment, and self-esteem to psychological health. In conclusion, all three analyses confirmed that the relationship between each attachment variable and adolescent depression was primarily mediated by self-esteem. Symister & Friend (2003) linked social support to depression entirely through low self-esteem and Roberts and colleagues (1996) determined that self-esteem moderated the relationship between insecure adult attachment and depressive symptoms in a sample of patients with chronic disease. In their investigation of career indecision in young adults, Smith and Betz (2002) implemented path models to conclude that self-esteem predicted depressed mood. Cheng and Furnham (2003) also used path analysis to report that self-esteem positively predicted happiness and positive affect and negatively predicted depression, dissatisfaction, and eating disorders. Finally, a study of 1,037 injured workers found that self-esteem attenuated the effect of physical injury on depression (Seff et al. 1992).

3.6. Parent-Adolescent Relationships and Adolescent Self-Esteem

Although numerous studies have established the significance of parent-child relationships in predicting both adolescent self-esteem and depressed mood, few have disentangled the interconnected linkages between the emotional states. The present investigation analyzes the processes by which parent-child relationship domains may contribute to adolescents' depressive states by incorporating self-esteem as a potential mediating variable.

Intimate connections with significant others are established as vital to adolescent self-esteem (O'Koon 1997; Roberts & Bengtson 1993). More specifically, children's perceptions of parental appraisals are consistently shown to be the most powerful predictors of self-esteem and self-evaluation in children (Carlson et al. 2000; DuBois et al 1998; Rubin et al.). Care, warmth, and support received from significant figures are shown to positively reinforce an individual's sense of worth. Especially for teenagers coping with new challenges of identity negotiation, parental appraisals become particularly important (Baltes & Silverberg 1994; Gecas & Schwalbe 1986). Identity theory depicts adolescence as a time of heightened self-awareness and self-consciousness about how one is perceived by others (Harter 1990; Simmons & Rosenberg 1975). Ironically, attachment relationships with parents are critical to adolescents who are disaffiliating from parents in their development of competent, worthy, and autonomous selves (Noom et al. 1999).

Literature on mattering is particularly pertinent to studies of self-concept formation since parents transmit fundamental information to children via perceived appraisals, which are used by children to evaluate their sense of inherent worth. Mattering, defined as the extent to which we feel we make a difference to the people and world around us, suggests that individuals who believe they matter to significant others feel socially relevant and worthy (Rosenberg & McCullough 1981). The theory of reflected appraisals supports that feeling cared for, needed by, and important to parents should be reflected in adolescents' views of how valuable they are to the world around them (Mead 1934). Internalizing a sense of personal significance and value in significant others' lives has been shown to facilitate positive feelings toward one's self, thereby enhancing self-esteem and protecting against depression (Elliott et al. 2004; Rosenberg & McCullough 1981; Taylor & Turner 2001). Conversely, feeling unimportant or irrelevant in the lives of significant others can be devastating to one's sense of social worth and can eventually lead to self-perceptions of worthlessness and low self-esteem (Rosenberg & McCullough 1981). Therefore, parents who are actively involved in children's lives and convey love and interest to children effectively promote self-esteem. This book contends that an adolescent's perceived attachment to a respective parental figure shapes mood disturbance primarily through the parent's influence on the adolescent's sense of self. Through close, warm, and involved relationships children internalize positive reflected appraisals that enhance self-worth and self-esteem.

Based on literature substantiating the mediating role that self-esteem plays in the development of depressive symptoms as well as the established significance of parents to children's self-concept, I anticipate that self-esteem will be a powerful mediator between parent-adolescent relations and depressive symptomatology. Further, in concert with earlier hypotheses pertaining to adolescent depressed mood, parental attachment is expected to be more salient to children's sense of selves than parental involvement.

3.6.1. Phase I: Hypotheses 4 and 5

H4. Most of the association between parent-adolescent relationship domains and adolescent depressed mood should be explained by the mediation of adolescent self-esteem.

H5. Self-esteem should be a stronger mediator in the relationship between dyadic parent-adolescent attachment and depressed mood than the relationship between parental involvement and depressed mood.

3.7. Gender-Specific Sources of Adolescent Self-Esteem

Although adolescent development is challenging for both boys and girls, research has consistently found lower levels of self-esteem among adolescent girls as compared to adolescent boys (Avison & McAlpine 1992; Chubb & Fertman 1997; Quatman & Watson 2001). Most likely, gender discrepancies in adolescent depressed mood originate from divergent self-esteem levels among male and female adolescents. One of the primary aims of this book is to illustrate how the pervasive influence of gender affects the sources and outcomes of adolescent self-esteem.

Psychological centrality is relevant to issues of self-esteem since notions of what people consider to be important impact the sources they utilize to define and judge themselves in relations to others. As mentioned previously, research illustrates that female self-concepts tend to be linked to emotional support, intimate relationships, and self-definition while male self-concepts are most dependent on achievement, status, and self-attribution (Eder & Hallihan 1978; Lord & Eccles 1994; Nottleman 1987; Verkuyten 2003). For example, in accordance with societal gender scripts, girls are found to care more about reflected appraisals or others' views of them while boys are believed to be more concerned with how they compare to others (Kling et al. 1999). When adolescents negotiate their identities in relation to others, such gender orientations become extremely salient.

Cross & Madson (1997) assert that culture shapes the processes by which individuals define and validate themselves. The authors distinguish males from females as respectively embodying independent self-construals, in which autonomy is sought for self-verification, from interdependent self-contruals, in which the self is defined through connectedness with others. In this perspective, male self-esteem is usually based on individualistic goals and differentiating oneself from others while female self-esteem enhancement depends on self-defining relationships and intimacy with others. Via a connection of vicarious involvement, even parental relationships with others, with spouses for instance, can indirectly affect the self-esteem of children with interdependent self-construals (Markus & Kitayama 1991).

3.7.1. Parent-Child Gender Dyads

Relations with parents are found to impact children's self-esteem in gender distinct ways. Barber and Thomas (1986) found maternal support and paternal affection to be correlated with daughters' self-esteem while maternal companionship and paternal presence was most significant to sons' self-esteem. In addition, O'Koon (1997) reported that mother-adolescent attachment was associated with children's ability to cope with failure while father-adolescent attachment was linked to general mastery and confidence. This latter finding is consistent with a growing body of research that links maternal influences to children's expressive outcomes and paternal influences to children's instrumental outcomes (Cabrera et al. 2000; Scanzoni 1991; Starrels 1992).

Still, a preponderance of literature has emphasized the importance of same-sex parent-child relations to children's self-esteem (Blos 1985; Crockenberg et al. 1996; Liu 2003; Maccoby 1994). Due to intense self-consciousness, the need for gender verification, and enormous pressure to prescribe to societal gender roles, teens are found to be more dependent on appraisals from same-sex parents. In accordance with my earlier hypotheses, I expect interpersonal connections with same-sex parents to be more significant to adolescent self-esteem than cross-sex parent-adolescent relations.

Contemporary psychoanalysis corroborates principles of gender-specific psychological centrality. As referenced earlier, Chodorow's identification theory highlights young girls' deep connections with their mothers, which instills in them a need to retain interpersonal connections for their sense of selves (Chodorow 1974, 1978). The theory further illustrates boys' rejection of mother-son intimacy in their search for less available fathers. Consequently, female self-concepts tend to be based on personal connections with others while male self-concepts are more likely to be derived from individuality. Based on theoretical perspectives of primary filial feminine identification and female orientation toward reflected appraisals and connectedness, I hypothesize that girls should be most vulnerable to perceptions of same-sex and opposite-sex parental relations than boys. Moreover, of all parent-child dyads I expect mother-daughter relationships to be most vital to adolescent self-esteem.

3.7.2. Phase I: Hypotheses 6 through 8

H6. Same-sex parent-adolescent relationship attachment and involvement should be stronger predictors of adolescent self-esteem than cross-sex parent-adolescent relationship domains.

H7. Same-sex and cross-sex parent-adolescent relations should be more predicative of girls' self-esteem than boys' self-esteem.

H8. Of all dyadic parent-adolescent relations, those between mothers and daughters should exhibit the strongest association with self-esteem outcomes.

3.8. Mediation of Academic Achievement

Adolescent educational achievement is not only valuable to future academic and professional success, but it is reported to have important influences on adolescent emotional well-being. While many studies show clear correlation between academic performance and adolescent self-worth (Owens 1994), others have attempted to extrapolate bidirectional findings through longitudinal analyses. For example, Schmidt and Padilla (2003) found that good school grades enhanced self-esteem.

3.8.1. Academic Achievement and Self-Esteem

Studies examining the relationship between academic achievement and self-esteem have conclusively exhibited a clear and significant association between the two variables. However, when it comes to pinpointing the directionality of that association, research remains inconsistent. Regardless, both camps are backed by strong advocates. The belief that self-esteem boosts academic achievement has prompted national school programs aimed at improving academic success by raising students' self-esteem. Such self-esteem models are based on the principle that high self-esteem improves academic grades through positive self-beliefs. However, such programs have been largely unsuccessful overall. For example, in 1986 California state legislators initiated a bill to promote adolescent self-esteem in order to fend off negative consequences such as drug abuse, teen pregnancy and low academic performance (State of California 1986). However, the task force commissioned to establish a causal link between self-esteem and academic competency failed to do so. Many scholars actually affirm that, if anything, higher self-esteem lowers academic success citing that individuals with high self-regard have little motivation to exert extra effort to obtain higher grades (Hewitt 1998).

Cross-cultural studies also caution that self-esteem does not predict academic performance. In Stevenson and Stigler's 1992 comparison of Asian and American elementary students' academic skills, the Asian students demonstrated significantly higher academic competency. Yet when students were asked to evaluate their own academic expertise, the American students perceived themselves to have much higher academic efficacy. The authors concluded that while Asian teachers rewarded students for academic mastery and considered academic mistakes important pedagogical guiding principles, teachers in the U.S. were overly sensitive and avoided recognizing children's academic failures for fear that errors in performance would damage their self-esteem.

In sum, the strongest empirical evidence supports that academic success promotes self-esteem, but rejects that self-esteem elevates scholastic performance. In this way, students who achieve scholastically feel good about their efforts and develop a sense of mastery over personal successes and failures, thereby enhancing self-esteem (Baumeister et al. 2003; DuBois et al. 1998; Rosenberg et al. 1989; Ross & Broh 2000).

3.8.2. Academic Achievement and Depression

Empirical evidence indicates that children who feel they can meet academic demands and have control over scholastic success have bolstered efficacy to resist depressive affect (Bandura et al. 1996). In a study of college students, respondents exhibited transitory depressive symptomatology during examination periods (Surtees et al. 2002). More specifically, Little and Garber (2004) found that regardless of academic orientation, females' mental health was impaired when confronted with newfound academic stress while boys exhibited aggressive behavior in the face of comparable stresses. All in all, research implies that the relationship between academic success or failure and enduring depressive symptoms is mediated by self-esteem. Few studies have affirmed direct linkage between academic achievement and depressed mood.

3.9. Parent-Adolescent Relationships and Academic Achievement

In order to disentangle the familial processes that lead to children's academic success or failure, much research has drawn on social capital models. As discussed in the theoretical section of this book, children obtain an array of resources from their relationships with significant others, namely parents. Accordingly, loving and supportive childrearing that values communication and involvement is critical in providing children with social capital, which fosters academic competency and motivates children to achieve in the classroom (Coleman 1988; Dornbusch 1989; Greenberg et al. 1983). Therefore, parents who have high expectations for children, but fail to invest adequate levels of social capital in them should have difficulty transmitting those expectations onto children. In order for teenagers to internalize and desire goals similar to their parents, social capital must be invested.

Parental educational attainment, along with the various resources educated parents tend to provide for their offspring, is considered a predominant determinant of academic-oriented resources children receive (Bianchi & Robinson 1997). Nevertheless, research has pointed to the complexity of familial capital's role in children's academic outcomes. For instance, McNeal (1999) found parental involvement to be inversely associated with children's school absences and likelihood to drop out, but did not find significant association in regard to the cognitive outcome of science achievement. In other analyses, parental socioeconomic status (White & Glick 2000) and mother's educational expectations (Coleman 1988) were shown to minimize risks of dropping out of high school.

Students who are raised in households consisting of two biological parents tend to fare better academically than children reared in single parent or stepfamily households (Astone & McLanahan 1991; Krein & Beller 1988; Sun & Li 2001). Given that the current sample's respondents resided in intact family households, they should have higher than average grade point averages.

Social cognitive theory offers a framework for parental impact on children's cognitive competency that is very similar, but conceptual different from that of social capital models. Social cognitive models posit that a child's upbringing fosters various levels of self-regulatory capabilities, self-beliefs, and aspirations that are continually developed by children themselves. Parents who communicate strict standards of behavior and expectations to children, but who are also supportive and loving, are found to benefit children's future academic success the most. For instance, while parental involvement and authoritativeness have been found to positively influence staying in school (White & Glick 2000) and academic achievement (Cabrera 2000; Dornbusch et al. 1987; Portes 2000; Steinberg et al. 1989), neglectful and overindulgent childrearing have both been associated with lower academic grades (Cohen & Rice 1997; Dornbusch et al. 1987; Glasgow et al. 1997).

3.10. Gender-Specific Sources of Adolescent Academic Achievement

On average, boys and girls present very different levels of academic competency and accomplishment. As a whole, girls attain higher secondary school grades and graduation rates than boys. While girls tend to achieve better grades in English and language arts courses, boys are shown to surpass girls in math despite the fact that this latter gap is narrowing (Eccles et al. 1991, 2002). Still, since the 1990's girls have been outperforming boys in the classroom at considerable rates. Males are 30% more likely to drop out of high school than female peers (Conlin 2003) and men are now outnumbered by women on college campuses. Of undergraduate college enrollment, men currently makeup 44% of student bodies nationally as compared to 58% three decades ago (Tyre 2006). In fact, statisticians predict a complete reversal in Bachelor of Arts degrees earned by year 2020, in which women are forecasted to graduate with 61% of all BA degrees (Conlin 2003).

The academic tribulations of young males have been attributed to biological deficiencies, in which boys' brains and emotions are hypothesized to make complex thinking and impulse control exceedingly difficult (Gurian & Ballew 2003). As a matter of fact, boys are twice as likely as girls to be diagnosed with attention-deficit or attention-deficit hyperactivity disorder. Environmental factors have also been examined. Increased divorce and lack of father figures, sensory-stimulating video games, and unsavory male role models are all conjectured to be contributors to boys' scholastic lagging. Others contend that while federal initiatives such as Title IX and the "Girl Project" of the 1990's helped girls achieve in classrooms and on playing field across the nation, boys were largely ignored. Defenders of male adolescents' academic plight criticize classroom environments that cater to female traits (Burke & Reitzes1981; Kindlon & Thompson 2000). Elementary and secondary school classrooms tend to emphasize a structured pedagogy that refrains movement and necessitates quiet, attentive, and disciplined behavior, all of which correspond with girls' feminine dispositions and conflict with boys' masculine personalities. Burke (1989) even conceives of a "semantic congruence" in which school itself is more feminine and thus more aligned with role identities of female teenage students than male counterparts.

High school is now more academically challenging than ever before. Ever-increasing standardized test requirements and cutthroat college acceptance competition add mounting pressure for all students, but especially for those falling behind. Given the importance of educational achievement to the social and professional futures of all adolescents, it is critical to understand the extent to which adolescent gender and academic achievement influence adolescent selves.

3.10.1. *Parent-Adolescent Gender Dyads*

Child development research has uncovered discrepancies between paternal and maternal influences on boys' and girls' academic performance. Father's involvement, in particular, has been linked to children's intellectual development and school achievement (Amato 1994; Cabrera 2000; Flouri & Buchanan 2003). Mortimer (1986) linked paternal support with occupational attainment and Mulkey and colleagues (1992) found that children without available fathers scored lower on academic and cognitive tests than counterparts with accessible father figures.

In order to decipher the sex-specific sources of children's scholastic motivations, theories of resource control and social power are valuable. Both theories deviate from sex-role theories of identification, which emphasize gender socialization and acquisition to instead focus on control of power. According to the resource control theory, the parent most in control of valued resources becomes a main source of children's imitative behavior (Bandura et al, 1963; Maccoby & Jacklin 1974). The theory further specifies that the value of such resources is based on children's evaluations.

More pertinent, however, are social power models of parental identification, which posit that the more power a parent is perceived to possess, the more likely a child will identify with that parent (Smith 1970; McDonald 1977, 1980). By way of two studies, McDonald established that the relationship between parental power and children's identification was stronger for fathers than mothers (McDonald 1977, 1980). More specifically, McDonald reported that daughters were more influenced by fathers than were sons. Referent power, or a parent's ability to impart guidance or advice, was found to be the most salient form of parental power for children. Expert power, based on parental competence or knowledge, followed by legitimate power, or the child's perception of a parent's right to control his or her opinions or behavior, were cited as other influential types of parental social power. Although Acock & Yang (1984) criticize McDonald for overlooking halo effects, in which a child's identification with one parent is transferred to the other parent, they nonetheless concur that social power dimensions tend to be stronger predictors of a daughter's identification than a son's identification.

I expect dimensions of parental power to be predominant sources of relevancy for children's scholastic achievement. Unlike the affective components of depression and self-esteem, the educational domain is instrumental in nature. Due to social status beliefs that tie instrumental abilities with males and expressive traits with women (Marini 1990; Scanzoni 1972), children should be more inclined to attribute academic-oriented power to fathers than mothers. In effect, children should be predisposed to view fathers, rather than mothers, as dominant authority figures and competent advisors of educational choices.

Furthermore, although prior hypotheses have predicted that parent-adolescent attachment would be most salient to children's affective components of mental health, namely self-esteem and depressed mood, I expect parental involvement to be most salient to children's instrumental competencies, specifically scholastic success. Aforementioned social capital models support that involved parents are particularly important to children's cognitive achievement.

3.10.2. *Phase I: Hypotheses 9 through 11*

H9. Academic achievement should partially mediate the association between parent-adolescent relationship domains and adolescent self-esteem.

H10. Academic achievement should more powerfully mediate the relationship between dyadic parent-adolescent involvement and self-esteem than parental attachment and self-esteem.

H11. Adolescents' relationships with fathers should be more significant to academic outcomes than relationships with mothers.

3.11. Secondary Analyses

Indeed, as an actor within a context of interrelated micro and macro level settings, an adolescent's developing self-concept is shaped by many sources (Bronfenbrenner, 1979). Although it would be impossible for the present analysis to investigate fully the myriad of factors that likely influence adolescents' emerging identities, notable variables were examined. These secondary variables assess adolescent and familial demographics as well as other factors found to influence adolescents' states of being, such as those relating to interpersonal relationships and school involvement.

Parental Educational Attainment: Overall, research findings examining the association between family socioeconomic status and adolescents' emotional outcomes have ranged from negative (Soares & Soares, 1969), insignificant (Epps, 1969), to modestly positive (Demo & Savin-Williams, 1983; Ensminger et al., 2000). Despite the fact that numerous studies have correlated socioeconomic status with emotional and cognitive outcomes, peripheral influences challenge the validity of direct and significant association (Parcel & Meneghan, 1993; Rosenberg & Pearlin 1978). For example, in 2003 Goodman and colleagues sampled 15,112 adolescents to conclude that low household income and low parental educational attainment accounted for one-third of respondents' depression and obesity. However, authors cautioned that estimates may have been overestimated on account of numerous proximal risk factors that affected socioeconomic status.

Other researchers have found significant differential effects of socioeconomic status associated with adolescent age. In 1978, Rosenberg and Pearlin discovered that the effect of social class on self-esteem varied by age and reported no association for children, modest association for adolescents, and significant association for adults. In support of results, authors deduced that comparison groups tended to be more homogeneous for youth than adults, that social class was indicative of achieved success among adults but not children, and that socioeconomic status was not psychologically central or important to the lives of typical children or adolescents. Later, Demo and Savin-Williams (1983) partially supported the well-known findings by concluding that social class was more significant to eighth graders than fifth graders by citing increased awareness of status with age. In sum, both studies provided evidence that social class becomes more predicative of self-esteem with age.

Using path models, Ross and Huber (1985) corroborated the importance of psychological centrality by finding that husbands' personal earnings provided protection from depression while wive's own earnings showed no direct effect. The authors concluded that wives considered their earnings to be supplemental while husbands assumed the role of primary breadwinner, thus making salary more salient to the self-worth of husbands than wives.

Whitbeck and colleagues' 1991 study revealed inconsistencies in earlier research. The authors found that the association between familial financial hardship and adolescent self-esteem was fully moderated by decreased parental support and involvement. By ascertaining only indirect association between parental socioeconomic status and child well-being, the findings stressed the need to control for parent-child relationship variables. For example, it is important to recognize that parents' level of education should certainly alter child-rearing styles and, therefore, the impact of parental education should be partially captured in the central parental relationship variables (Stright & Bales 2003; Wong et al. 2002).

Theories of socialization, which contend that males learn to be more competitive and status-oriented than females, suggest that family socioeconomic status should be more influential to the identity and emotional health of male adolescents than female adoelscents. On the other hand, Bem's self-perception theory, which proposes that it is personal behavior and achievement that shapes human self-concept and not others' successes or failures, offers a much different perspective (Bem 1967). Since parental socioeconomic status is ascribed and not achieved by the adolescent him or herself, self-perception theorists surmise that ascribed status is not likely to be internalized as part of an adolescent's self-concept.

However, through educational attainment parents develop human capital, which has consistently been shown to provide important resources that enhance children's academic success (White & Glick 2000). More specifically, parental involvement in children's school related activities and parental expectations for children's intellectual attainment are powerful predictors of children's academic competency (Bogenschneider 1997; Coleman 1988; Portes 2000; White & Glick 2000). According to such hypotheses, academic success should raise self-esteem which, in turn, should lower risks for depressed mood. If this process proves to be at work in the present analysis, the impact of parental education will be greatly weakened by the primary explanatory variables.

Compiling the vast but inconsistent scholarly and theoretical work associated with familial socioeconomic status and adolescent psychosocial outcomes is challenging. Nevertheless, considering that parental educational attainment is ascribed and not achieved, I do not expect perceptions of parental educational status to be directly significant to adolescents' self views. Instead, given that parental education yields various forms of social capital, which are passed onto children both implicitly and explicitly, higher levels of parental education should offer some cognitive and emotional benefits to children. Well both maternal and paternal educational attainment should positively influence adolescent well-being overall, the education of same-sex parents should be most salient to adolescents' psychological health. That is to say that given the significance of same-sex parents to adolescents' identity development, children should readily model same-sex parents in defining own expectations.

However, in the domain of academic achievement, paternal educational status should be more influential than maternal educational status. According to resource and social power models, children are more likely to attribute legitimate and referential power to fathers, who represent the instrumental parental role, and expert power to mothers, who play the expressive role within families (Scanzoni 1991; Starrels 1992). Given the instrumentality of scholastic achievement, children should favor fathers over mothers as academic role models. In conclusion, parental education is expected to have stronger effects on the instrumental component of academic achievement than the affective components of self-esteem and depressed mood. Still, it is important to recognize that much of the effect of parental education should be absorbed by parent-teen relationships, thus curbing its significance.

Maternal Employment Status: In addition to parental education, I assessed mothers' employment status. U.S. Department of Labor estimates from 1987, the time period in which the cohort of respective respondents were preadolescents, reported that 71% of married mothers with children aged 6 to 17 were employed. Yet, research of working mothers' impact on families is both relatively new and inconsistent. Thorough examinations have found inconsistent effects of mother's employment status on children's cognitive and emotional well-being ranging from negative (Hoffman 1980) to positive (Furstenberg 1995; Heyns 1982). Gold & Andres (1978) reported that working mothers benefited children's social competence and independence and in a 1995 longitudinal analysis of high school students, Muller concluded that children with mothers who worked part time achieved the highest gains in mathematics. The single consistent finding to emerge in research on maternal employment and children's psychological and academic competency has concluded that sporadic maternal employment patterns as well as a mother's dissatisfaction with her job adversely affect children's well-being (Burchinal & Rossman 1961; Heyns & Catsambis 1986).

Scholarly work that has investigated whether maternal employment influences male and female children differently is also sparse and inconclusive. Worth mentioning, however, is Booth and Amato's 1994 study that linked employed mothers with positive psychosocial and academic outcomes for daughters, but negative academic consequences for sons. Spitze's 1988 review of employed mothers cited sex-role modeling to surmise that daughters of employed mothers were more likely to be independent, studious, and forward-thinking regarding their own future careers. Though Spitze also concluded that boys with employed mothers performed worse in school than boys with stay-at-home mothers, she underscored that this corresponded to middle-class families only.

Despite inconsistent literature, the greatest influence of maternal employment on daughters should be filtered through same-sex modeling while the bulk of effects for sons should be associated with social capital and availability. As a whole, maternal employment is not expected to have considerable influence on children's emotional psyches or academic achievement as both outcomes should primarily be associated with mother's attachment, involvement, and educational attainment.

Developmental Age: As discussed previously, the majority of child developmental research has recognized early adolescence, or 12 to 14 years old, as signifying the height of self-concept disturbance. By mid-adolescence, or 15 to 17 years of age, most teenagers are thought to begin to feel more comfortable as individuals, and during late adolescence, or 18 to 19 years of age, secure identities are believed to materialize. Research suggests that parent-child attachment begins to decline significantly during early adolescence, resulting in both increased autonomy and detachment stress for children. Buist and colleagues (2002) investigated processes of same-sex parent deidealization to find that children's attachment to same-sex parents tended to decline steadily throughout the adolescent period (ages 11-17) while cross-sex parent-child attachment failed to exhibit consistent pathways. For example, boys exhibited intense detachment from mothers during early adolescence (ages 11-13) but showed no clear trends thereafter while father-daughter attachment displayed a steep, but later onset decline in early adolescence, but revealed closer subsequent attachment. Overall, the authors concluded that same-sex attachment was more prominent than opposite-sex attachment.

School transitions add another component to the impact of school grade or age on adolescent emotional and cognitive development. Upon the transition to a new school, coping with unfamiliar, larger environments can be quite traumatic for maturing adolescents (Barber & Olsen 2004; Blyth et al. 1978; Crockett et al. 1989; Lord & Eccles 1994; Fenzel 2000). Simmons et al. (1973) proclaimed that environment was more predicative of psychosocial disturbance than age by finding that junior high schoolers had poorer self-image than same-aged children in elementary school. Little and Garber (2004) explicated such contextual research by concluding that only girls with high interpersonal orientations were likely to become depressed when faced with peer stressors in new high school environments. Such findings indicate that girls may be more susceptible to psychological impairment associated with changes in school environment than boys.

Adolescent Race-Ethnicity: Given the paramount role of race and ethnicity to self-identification, this study controlled for respondents' racial-ethnic identity. Studies examining the effects of race and ethnicity on self-concept formation, and particularly depressive risks, are relatively new. Since the 1990's research has affirmed that culture, race, and ethnicity play significant roles in the behavioral outcomes of teens and, hence, should be accounted for in any study of adolescent well-being (Lerner et al. 1999; McAdoo 1999; Schwartz & Montgomery 2002; Steinberg 2001; Verkuyten 2003).

Strong ethnic ties, group integration, and cultural socialization are all associated with positive sense of selves (Gray-Little & Hafdahl 2000; Phinney et al. 1999; Umana-Taylor et al. 2002). In contrast, it is plausible that an adolescent who rejects or feels shame toward his or her ethnicity should suffer psychological distress and adverse effects to self-esteem. In their examination of African American and Mexican American youth, Phinney & Devich-Navarro (1997) found that those adolescents who maintained connections with both mainstream American culture as well as respective cultures of heritage fared best psychologically. Cultural upbringing is a factor that has unquestionable influence over one's self-concept. Traditional patriarchal ideologies, for example, have been linked to decreased self-esteem in girls (Carlson et al. 2000).

Most analyses support that African American children have higher self-esteem than White, Asian American, Native American, and Latino peers (Hughes & Demo 1989; Rotheram-Borus et al. 1996; Steinberg 2001). Even though some research has reported no association between race and self-esteem, such reports are vastly outnumbered (Wade 1991). I expect race to impact adolescents regardless of gender since it has such broad implications for status, belonging, and cultural ideology.

Immigrant status is also incorporated in the present analysis since being an immigrant in an American school system is likely to engender unique developmental experiences. Research on immigrant adolescents has most often focused on culture, both the maintenance of native culture and assimilation into American culture. While intuitive reasoning would suggest that immigrants would have greater difficulty during adolescence, the reverse has in fact been reported. Harker (2001) utilized Add Health data to find that first-generation, but not second-generation, immigrants experienced significantly less depressive affect and more positive well-being than American counterparts. She attributes greater well-being to protective and supportive familial systems.

Adolescent Religiosity: Surprisingly, very few studies have examined the relationship between religion and adolescent cognitive and emotional outcomes. Although some research suggests that religion provides believers with emotional support, inner tranquility, and personal fulfillment (Schapman & Inderbitzen 2002), other findings discount association between religion and psychological health (Markstrom 1999). The concept of psychological centrality supports that the more importance a person places on religion, the more central religion should be to his or her identity and, consequently, should be of greater psychological significance. In a study of 3,356 adolescent girls, Miller and Merav (2002) reported that personal devotion and religious community were correlated with a 19-43% reduction in depressive symptomatology, which fluctuated based on the respondent's level of maturity.

Participation in religious activities and connection to a church is thought to provide access to social networks of interpersonal relationships with others who hold similar moral viewpoints (Rohrbaugh & Jessor 1975). Durkheimian philosophy contends that religiosity is an important source of social integration, which serves as a protective factor against emotional trauma and suicidal thoughts (Durkheim 1915; Salmons & Harrington 1984; Stack 1983). Zhang and Jin (1996) unearthed perplexing cultural differentials in their structural equation analysis of religiosity and the psychological outcomes of depression, suicide ideation, pro-suicide attitudes. Results demonstrated significant negative association between religiosity and the variables among Americans, but significant positive association among the Chinese sample. The authors attributed the disparate results to China's religious culture that began as a "deviant behavior in the economically and ideologically reformed" country. Given the overabundance and diversity of religions and religious congregations, one can surmise that not all levels of religiosity offer the same personal sanctity and satisfaction.

On average, and regardless of denomination, I expect religion to provide believers with spiritual encouragement, inner tranquility, and personal fulfillment (Schapman & Inderbitzen 2002). Religiosity was expected to be linked to female, but not male, psychosocial health due to females' tendency to place more emphasis on emotional support.

Sibling Composition: In order to account for the full complexity of family dynamics, my analysis also accounts for presence of siblings. Granted, little academic evidence exists to confirm that sibling composition directly affects other siblings' emotional or cognitive outcomes. Even so, the resource dilution hypothesis is most often cited to theorize intra-sibling influences. Arising from neo-classical economic theories and often incorporated in social capital theory, the resource dilution model abides by the basic premise that "child quality competes with child quantity (Blake 1981, 1985)". Accordingly, each additional sibling sucks parental attention away from a respective child, thereby diluting the social and financial capital investment allotted. In corroboration of such theory, literature has suggested that having siblings adversely affects a child's academic potential (Downey 1995; Steelman et al. 2002) and attention received from parents (Harris & Morgan 1991; Hofferth et al. 1988). Exemplifying its economic origins, resource dilution not only assumes finite parental investments, but also disregards social capital gained by sibling relationships themselves.

Recent research of sibling relationships indicates that siblings provide important social support and contribute to the self-esteem and academic competency of brothers and sisters (Jodl et al. 1999). However, the majority of studies that have concluded significant association between number of siblings and lowered self-esteem have only been able to do so indirectly through decreased parental support and involvement (Kidwell 1981; McHale et al. 2000; Parcel & Meneghan 1993; Tucker et al. 2003). Sibling relations are believed to become less significant as adolescents form close friendships in non-family contexts. Research findings, albeit minimal, showing that siblings do in fact impact the emotional well-being of one another, suggest that it is necessary to control for sibling composition (Kidwell 1981).

Adolescent Body Weight: Adolescent weight, operationalized through body mass index, has been shown to impact both female and male adolescent psyches. America's obsession with food and weight has had harmful implications for our nation's youth in two distinctive ways. First, American children, who are larger and more unhealthy than ever before, have become a particularly disconcerting component of the current obesity epidemic. Due to increased consumption of food high in sugar and fat along with decreased activity, the proportion of overweight children aged 12-19 has skyrocketed from 5% in the period of 1976-1980 to over 16% in the period between 1999 and 2002 (Centers for Disease Control 2003). If current trends continue, nearly half of children in North and South America will be overweight within the decade (Furse 2006). Of this group, the children most at risk for being overweight include non-Hispanic Black females (24.7%) and Mexican-American males (27%) (Centers for Disease Control 2003). Based on national survey data of 9th to 12th graders, the Centers for Disease Control and Prevention further reported that 26.9% of males and 40.1% of females fail to get adequate exercise[1]. Of particular concern is the fact that childhood and adolescent obesity do not appear to be ephemeral. In a recent study, the Centers for Disease Control reported that 65% of adults were overweight and, of those, 46% were obese (Centers for Disease Control 2002).

Beyond the obvious health risks associated with obesity, such as diabetes, being overweight is associated with numerous psychosocial problems as well. For instance, overweight status can cause extreme angst and anxiety as well as heightened states of self-consciousness. For female adolescents in particular, stressors associated with overweight status have been linked to depressed mood (Needham & Crosnoe 2005) and self-esteem (Pesa et al. 2000). Still, nationally representative studies have found abnormal weight status to be associated with negative adjustment and psychosocial disturbance among adolescent girls as well as boys (Ge et al. 2001; Goodman & Whitaker 2002).

Crosnoe and Muller's 2004 longitudinal study of adolescents at risk for obesity reported that respondents were susceptible to poor academic achievement. Findings were particularly relevant in school environments that stigmatized overweight peers, typically schools with higher rates of romantic activity and lower mean body size.

The second dangerous offshoot of contemporary U.S. culture's obsession with food and bodies is the soaring prevalence of eating disorders. In our aesthetically

---

[1] Recommended physical activity for high school students, based on *Healthy People 2010*, is defined as at least five or more days per week of thirty minutes of moderate exercise (doesn't require sweating or hard breathing) or three or more days per week of at least twenty minutes of vigorous activity (causes sweating or hard breathing).

conscious society beauty has become a highly coveted status symbol. Advertising, media, and cosmetic industries only further perpetuate beauty myths by ensuring that unrealistically thin and flawless female bodies and chiseled male physiques gloss magazine covers and pervade television screens. Airbrushed magazine photos and cosmetic surgery generate unnatural images of males and females that come to represent cultural ideals.

Though unrealistic cultural standards of beauty clearly cross gender boundaries, feminist theory contends that such images are most dangerous for females, who suffer considerably more physical and emotional deterioration to self-image than males (Bordo 1993; Kilbourne 1995). Even comparing adolescents in the healthy weight range, girls were found to be significantly more likely than boys to feel discontented with their bodies (Casper & Offer 1990). Whitaker and colleagues (1989) found that 81% of an adolescent female sample wanted to lose weight despite the fact that 61% fell within the normal weight range. Appearance, particularly body image, has consistently been identified as a powerful contributor to teenage girls' self-esteem and depressed mood (Brooks-Gunn & Warren 1989; McDonald & Thompson 1992; Paxton et al. 1991; Usmiani & Daniluk 1997).

Adolescence marks a particularly difficult period for female body image. First, society attaches far greater importance on appearance as it relates to female identity than male identity. Second, during puberty female bodies inherently gain weight in the form of fat while males gain muscle mass. Hence, just as girls become most self-conscious during early adolescence, they are also gaining weight as they mature into women. Not surprisingly, girls are found to become most distressed about their bodies during early adolescence (Attie & Brooks-Gunn 1989; Wichstrom 1999).

Clear ethnic differences exist in regard to body image and psychosocial implications. For example, academics have recognized that, on average, Caucasian and African American female adolescents hold distinctive views of their bodies. African American girls report significantly higher levels of body satisfaction than their white counterparts (Brown et al. 1998; Parker et al. 1995; Simmons & Rosenberg 1975). Two cultural explanations are useful when probing this phenomenon. First, voluptuous female frames tend to be more desirable in African American culture as compared to Anglo Caucasian culture. Studying undergraduate college students, Klaczynski, Goold, and Mudry confirmed their hypothesis, which predicted that internalization of a "thin ideal" would mediate the relationship between weight and body esteem (Klaczynski et al. 2004). Second, as has been shown in cultural examinations, African American parents tend to socialize daughters to be independent and assertive while White or Asian parents are more apt to raise dependent and deferential daughters (Smith 1982; Way 1995). Such findings have been attributed to the marginalization of Black women in society and parental attempts to overcome this inequality. Girls who are more independent and self-assured clearly possess traits that help protect them from low self-worth and self-esteem. Additional research of ethnicity, gender, and appearance suggests that body image is significant to Hispanic and Asian American adolescent female emotional states, albeit not to the degree that it is to White females (Ge et al. 2001).

Although socioeconomic status does not appear to influence perceptions of body image for minorities, Dornbusch et al. (1984) found that familial income was positively associated with thin body ideals for White females. Similarly, while some negative emotional effects concerning body image have been linked to Caucasian males, African American and Hispanic males do not appear to be affected by their weight (Ge et al. 2001). Nonetheless, overweight and underweight statuses are expected to increase depressed mood and diminish self-esteem in both the male and female samples. However, the emotional consequences of abnormal body weight should be considerably more detrimental to girls than boys.

Extracurricular Participation: In the present analysis, I will examine respondents' involvement in extracurricular activities, specifically club and athletic participation. In general, youth activities are found to enhance feelings of school belonging (Anderman 2002) as well as provide adolescents with a unique opportunity for psychosocial development. Extracurricular activities are associated with a plethora of developmental benefits related to self-efficacy and self-esteem enhancement, identity exploration, emotional regulation, acquisition of teamwork and interpersonal skills, social networking, and scholastic success (Dworkin et al. 2003; Eccles et al. 2001; Fredricks et al. 2002; Hansen et al. 2003; Larson 2000; Schmidt & Padilla 2003). Extracurricular participation enables children to experience additional positive role identities, work and interact with same-aged peers, and confront challenges within a supportive environment independent of their parents (Eccles et al. 2002; Gilman 2001). Through extracurricular activities, adolescents volunteer to participate in interests that utilize and further develop the human capital they possess.

Club participation includes academic, musical, and leadership activities (e.g. debate club, Spanish club, band; see Appendix E). Students may choose to participate in clubs for a variety of reasons, such as improving collegiate appeal, experiencing related social benefits, or due to genuine interest. Given the voluntary nature of club involvement and considering that such participation is relatively stress-free, clubs are expected to have positive impact on adolescents' sense of selves. Not surprisingly, club participation is expected to be positively associated with academic achievement.

Athletics is the most expensive and popular extracurricular activity in U.S. secondary schools (Tracy & Erkut 2002; see Appendix F). Children join school sports teams primarily because sports are considered enjoyable. Schools cover the costs of sports for the sake of school spirit, for children's health and well-being, and because athletics has become an integral and expected component of school systems. In fact, according to a 2002 Centers for Disease Control and Prevention report, half of American students participate in school sports (Tracy & Erkut 2002).

The projected outcomes of high school athletic involvement run the gamut from negative to positive. Outcomes associated with athletics include heightened self-esteem, which has been attributed to physical activity itself (McAuley 1994) as well as athletic mastery (Maton 1990) and social identity acquisition (Eccles et al. 2001). Students who participate in athletics have been found to have better school grades and attendance than non athletes (Fejgin 1994; Videon 2002). For both boys and girls, and regardless of race, athletic success has been identified as the principal source of popularity in middle school and high school (Coleman 1961; Kennedy 1995, White et al. 1998). In fact, Gore and colleagues (2001) found that involvement in team sports protected adolescent females from depressed mood that was related to poor academic achievement.

Potential negative effects of high school sports involvement include stress and anxiety related to competition (Smoll & Smith 1996) and destructive physical or social pressure from coaches or teammates (Eccles & Barber 1999; Eder & Parker 1987). Given the masculine status bestowed upon athletes in our society, it is no surprise that sports are significantly more salient to males than females. Socialization theories that link primary relationships with female self-concepts and achievement-oriented activities with male self-concepts convey the importance of athletics for boys (Eccles et al. 1987; Hill & Lynch 1983; Shanahan et al. 1991). Unfortunately, the pressure placed on young male adolescents to be successful athletes can overstress the need to excel while disregarding the pure enjoyment of athletic participation. In addition, the competition involved in "making the cut" can intensify athletic-related stress. Still, possessing athletic status is highly coveted, especially for males and thus should be reflected in respondents' self-esteem. Therefore, despite negative consequences, athletic participation is expected to enhance self-esteem and protect against depressed mood, particularly for adolescent males.

Quality of Friendships: Given the increased dependence on friendships during adolescence, it was necessary to control for the quality of relationships with peers (Brown 1990; Mechanic & Hansell 1987). The transition to adolescence marks a period of increased parent-child conflict, albeit typically rather mild, in which adolescents and parents spend less time together (Larson & Richards 1991). However, in healthy parent-adolescent relationships such detachment allows adolescents increased independence and individual responsibility. The social maturation adolescents undergo enables them to establish relations with peers that are independent of their parents. While compensatory models suggest that peer relations become most desired by, and crucial to, adolescents who lack loving and caring parents, most current research advocates social cognitive models that regard parental and peer attachment as compliments to one another, such that high quality relationships with parents foster positive friendships (Wilkinson 2004).

Despite the fact that most evidence suggests that parent-teen attachment is more significant to children's long-term well-being than are attachments to peers (Armsden et al. 1990; Greenberg et al. 1983; Noom et al 1999; Raja et al. 1992; Wilkinson & Walford 2001), friendships nevertheless play a major role in adolescent development during adolescence. Through reciprocal relationships with same-aged peers children develop important social skills. Teenagers' friendships tend to mature from larger social groups in early adolescents to those that are more interpersonally connected by late adolescence (Gavin & Furman 1989). Throughout high school friends also become increasingly important to adolescents, who are thought to form relations based on shared understanding, loyalty, self-disclosure, and intimacy (Adler & Adler 1998; Bukowski et al. 1993; Hartup 1993; Lansford et al. 2003). In one study of 99 seventeen-year-old adolescents, three-quarters chose peers over parents as primary attachment figures (Freeman & Brown 2001). Not surprisingly, same-sex friends are more likely to be primary sources of companionship and personal communication than are opposite-sex friends (Lempers & Clark-Lempers 1992). Girls, in particular, value friends as reliable confidants (Youniss & Smollar 1985).

Children whose parents are warm and supportive and exemplify sociability themselves demonstrate higher levels of social competency than children whose parents are indifferent or anti-social. Human capital, in the form of parents' own social competence, as well as social capital, which signifies parental involvement in socializing offspring, impart invaluable resources that benefit children both implicitly and explicitly. In general, high quality parent-child relationships are thought to protect children from negative peer influences (Bogenschneider et al. 1998). On the other hand, children who lack caring and available parents are found to be more susceptible to peer pressure and delinquency (Gauze et al. 1996).

Regardless of whether parents impact children's choice of friends or not, the fact of the matter is that high quality friends play an integral role in nourishing confidence and prosocial behavior while poor quality friends can damage an adolescent's self-worth and can lead to destructive behavior (Jacob et al. 2004). For better or worse, Brown (1990) contends that middle adolescence is when children are most influenced by peers.

Overall, research has established that peers and peer groups impact adolescents' emotional well-being. Findings show that being a member of a popular or high-status group of friends is positively associated with self-esteem (Brown & Lohr 1987) while socially rejected adolescents are at risk for low self-esteem and depression (Rubin et al. 1995). Depressive symptomatology in teens is associated with increasing loneliness (Brage et al. 1995). While perceptions of having worthy friendships are expected to lower risks for depressed mood and boost self-esteem for the entire sample, friendships should be more salient to relationship-oriented females. However, the current project does not anticipate that friendships will impact adolescent academic performance.

Sexual Relations: This analysis will control for adolescents' romantic and non-romantic sexual relationships. Physical and emotional maturation as well as accompanying social pressures to acquire adult behaviors lead many adolescents to explore dating and romantic relationships. Experiencing opposite-sex romance is important considering the cultural expectations associated with ultimately finding a committed and supportive marital partner to share one's life with. Unfortunately, considering the relative immaturity of adolescents, romantic relations during this period are considerably more superficial, ephemeral, and unstable than adulthood romances.

Despite its recognized importance to adolescents, surprisingly little research has attempted to decipher the roles of romantic intimacy and sexual activity during the adolescent period (Furman et al.1999; Graber et al. 1996). Overall, empirical evidence seems to emphasize the negative emotional consequences of romance during adolescence. In the first nationally representative study of adolescent romantic relations and depression, Joyner and Udry (2000) surmised that both males and females who entered romantic relationships between longitudinal waves suffered higher rates of depressive affect than romantically uninvolved peers. Not surprisingly, intimate opposite-sex relationships adversely affected females to a greater extent than males. Theoretically, the salience of intimate connections to female self-concepts puts more pressure on girls to acquire romantic partners. Since reflected appraisals encountered from interpersonal others are thoroughly tied to female self-worth, breaking up with a romantic partner should be more damaging to female self-esteem than male self-esteem (Dyk & Adams 1990; Gilligan 1996).

The linkage between adolescent romance and sexual behavior make analyses exceedingly more complex. Though difficult to assess, varied estimates suggest that between 50-61% of American adolescents lose their virginity by the end of the developmental period and, furthermore, that rates of sexual activity are rising within this population (Kann et al. 1998; Lundberg & Plotnik 1990). Issues of sexuality cannot be examined without recognition of the cultural double standard, in which adolescent females who lose their virginity are often disrespected while adolescent males who are sexually experienced typically attain enhanced status. Girls internalize the pervasive and conflicting cultural message that they should be sexually attractive but not overtly sexual.

Studies examining the influences of adolescent sexual activity are nearly as scarce as research of adolescent romantic relationships. While some evidence has found association between adolescent sexual activity and psychological disturbance, other findings have shown no significant association. For example, Robinson & Frank (1994) found that neither virgin adolescent males nor virgin adolescent females had significantly higher or lower self-esteem than their nonvirgin counterparts. In contrast, other research has found a significant connection between the psychological components of low self-esteem and depression with sexually active females, but not males (Kowaleski-Jones & Mott 1998; Whitbeck et al. 1992). As a whole, longitudinal research supports that sexual activity precedes emotional psychopathology, having revealed only the weakest of causation in the inverse direction (Whitbeck et al. 1993).

Based on the literature review, it is my contention that sexual activity during adolescence should heighten depressed mood and deplete self-esteem in the adolescent female sample. Having been raped is expected to be most detrimental to adolescent female psychosocial outcomes, while non-romantic sexual encounters should generate greater emotional risks than sexual relations with romantic partners.

3.12. Longitudinal Analysis

The second phase of my project will incorporate a second wave of adolescent in-home interviews in order to assess the processes by which explanatory variables influence adolescent depressed mood over the course of one year. The longitudinal design is critical for thorough developmental examination. Assuming Phase I finds both variables to be significant mediators in the original relationship, one can infer that adolescent self-esteem and academic performance are both embedded in the processes that lead from parent-adolescent relations to depressive symptomatology.

Longitudinal analyses also examine adolescent self-esteem as well as each dyadic parent-adolescent relationship domain variable. In determining variable volatility, I regressed all explanatory variables (controlling for time 1 depressed mood) on time 2 depressed mood (Wave II). Findings provide insight into the causal influence of parent-child relations and other important variables on adolescent depressed mood over the course of one year. Next, I inserted time 1 self-esteem as the outcome variable and analyzed the relationships between all explanatory variables and changes to self-esteem. Additional longitudinal analyses examined each dyadic parent-teen relationship domain. First, I introduced time 2 mother-adolescent attachment as the sole dependent variable followed by father-adolescent attachment, maternal involvement, and paternal involvement. A total of twelve analyses were computed.

3.12.1.   Phase II, Longitudinal Hypotheses

H1. Time 1 adolescent depressed mood, adolescent self-esteem, parental attachment, and parental involvement variables should be significantly and positively associated with corresponding time 2 variables, thereby indicating stability over time.

H2. Time 1 parent-adolescent relationship domains, controlling for time 1 depressed mood, should be inversely associated with adolescent depressed mood at time 2.

H3. Time 1 parent-adolescent relationship domains, controlling for time 1 self-esteem, should be positively associated with adolescent self-esteem at time 2.

CHAPTER FOUR
DATA & METHODS

4.1. Data

This project utilized restricted-use data from the *National Longitudinal Survey of Adolescent Health* (Add Health), a nationally representative study that examined adolescent health-related behavior and psychological state (Udry 2003). The study aimed to examine the influences of various environmental contexts including schools, peers, families, and communities. Eighty high schools (88.8% public) of various metropolitan localities (52.5% suburban) and from every region of the country agreed to participate in the study. Participants included students, parents, siblings, peers, romantic partners, school administrators, and teachers. External data supplied supplemental information concerning neighborhoods and communities. Add Health is considered the "largest, most comprehensive survey of adolescents ever undertaken" (National Longitudinal Study of Adolescent Health 2003).

Throughout the 1994-1995 school year 90,118 seventh to twelfth grade boys and girls completed 45-minute in-school questionnaires. This first wave also included a random sample of 20,745 students from the larger in-school survey who completed in-home computer assisted personal interviews (CAPI) and audio computer assisted self interviews (ACASI). Wave I in-home interviews were conducted between April and December of 1995. In addition, parental questionnaires (N=17,700) were collected during the same period (April-December, 1995). 14,738 of the Wave I in-home adolescents were re-interviewed a year later between April and September of 1996 for a second longitudinal wave (71% retention). Most of the Wave I twelfth graders were excluded from the sample because they had graduated from high school. Although they were not used in this study, a third wave of interviews focused on developmental trajectories of the respondents when they were young adults four years after the second wave of interviews. The data are intended to assist scholars in analyzing adolescent issues and to produce research that will allow authorities to better understand and protect American teenagers.

The extensive nature of the data allowed me to evaluate a wide range of factors that have been shown to influence adolescent psychosocial well-being. The large sample size enabled me to eliminate cases in order to research only those adolescents residing with two married biological parents without sacrificing statistical potency. Moreover, I was able to exclude all questions with missing cases without impairing the analysis. The final sample consisted of 5,065 adolescents, 2,625 females and 2,440 males.

4.2. Variable Operationalization

4.2.1. *Dependent and Mediating Variables*

Adolescent Depressed Mood: The central dependent variable, adolescent depressed mood, was measured using 19 items from the Center for Epidemiological Studies Depression Scale (CES-D, Radloff 1977). CES-D scales are commonly used by practitioners to diagnose depression in children. Respondents were asked how often during the past week they felt various feelings or symptoms such as fearfulness, loneliness, or sadness (refer to Appendix B for complete list of questions). Responses included *never or rarely* (1), *sometimes* (2), *a lot of the time* (3), and *most of the time or all of the time* (4). The internal consistency reliability (Cronbach's alpha) for the depression measures were .87 and .88 for time 1 and time 2, respectively. The final adolescent depressed mood index, assessed at both Wave I and Wave II, ranges from 19 to 76.

Adolescent Self-Esteem: The first mediating variable, adolescent self-esteem, was measured using six questionnaire statements originally derived from Rosenberg's measures of general self-esteem (Rosenberg 1965). Items that were asked of respondents measured personal feelings of possessing good qualities, being prideful and content with oneself, social and instrumental competence, and feeling loved by others. Statements included, "you have a lot of good qualities", "you have a lot to be proud of", and "you like yourself just the way you are" (see Appendix C for complete listing). Answer choices were distributed along five-point Likert scales, which included *strongly disagree* (1), *disagree* (2), *neither agree nor disagree* (3), *agree* (4), and *strongly agree* (5). With the exception of "you have a lot to be proud of" at time 2, the statistical mode for all adolescent responses was *strongly agree*. The Cronbach's alpha for all six measures was .85 (time 1) and .87 (time 2) and the final index ranges from 5 to 30.

Adolescent Academic Achievement: Adolescent academic achievement was measured using adolescent self-reported grades for each respondent's most recent grading period. The first survey question asked, "at the {most recent grading period or last grading period in the spring}, what was your grade in English or language arts?" Afterward, each question simply asked, "and what was your grade in {mathematics/ history or social studies/ science}?" The grades for English, mathematics, history/social studies, and science, which include *A* (1), *B* (2), *C* (3), and *D or lower* (4), were inversely coded and then averaged for a final academic achievement mean. Subjects that respondents did not take at all or took but were not given a letter grade were excluded from the means computation. For example, if a student had a letter grade for English, math, and science but not history, their final mean for academic achievement would be based on three subjects, rather than four subjects. Mentally challenged adolescents were excluded from the analysis. Children were excluded from the survey if parents answered yes to the question, "is [your child] mentally retarded?"

4.2.2. Central Independent Variables

Central explanatory variables include mother-adolescent attachment and involvement, father-adolescent attachment and involvement, adolescent gender, and adolescent school grade. In the initial Phase I regression, a dichotomous gender variable defined each adolescent as male (reference) or female. Thereafter, adolescents were split by gender in separate regression analyses so that males were compared against females.

Parent-Adolescent Relationship Quality Variables: Maternal and paternal attachment and involvement were based on adolescents' survey answers. Research has consistently demonstrated that a child's and parent's perceptions of the same relationship differ considerably (Demo et al 1987; Gecas & Schwalbe 1986; Hartos & Power 2000). Considering that one's emotional state is shaped by one's own perceptions, adolescent views were used to assess parent-adolescent attachment as well as involvement. Only adolescents who resided with two married, biological parents were included in this analysis.

Parent-adolescent attachment was measured using teens' answers to the following survey questions, which were answered for each parent to evaluate children's relationships with mothers and fathers separately:

- Caring: How much do you think your mother/father cares about you?
- Closeness: How close do you feel toward your mother/father?
- Warmth: Most of the time your mother/father is warm and loving toward you.

Mother-daughter, mother-son, father-daughter, and father-son relationship measures produced alpha coefficients of .74, .64, .80 and .76, respectively. For the first two questions Likert answer options included *not at all* (1), *very little* (2), *somewhat* (3), *quite a bit* (4), and *very much* (5). The statement regarding parental warmth was also assessed using five options; *strongly agree* (1), *agree* (2), *neither agree nor disagree* (3), *disagree* (4), and *strongly disagree* (5). I reverse coded the latter statement in order to operationalize the scale from the most negative to the most positive assessment of parental warmth.

Not surprisingly, adolescents rated relationship attachment with both parents to be very high. On average, adolescents perceived stronger attachment to mothers than fathers. At time 1, 93% of adolescents felt their mothers cared very much while 87.8% felt their fathers cared very much. At time 2, respective percentages dropped slightly to 89.5% and 83.6%. Although parental closeness and warmth were not rated as highly as parental caring, most adolescents were still most likely to feel very close to mothers [68.7% (T1), 53.2% (T2)] and fathers [57.8% (T1), 42.2% (T2)]. Similarly, the majority of the sample perceived mothers [56.6% (T1), 52.3% (T2)] and fathers [44.1% (T1), 44.2% (T2)] to be warm and loving. Final relationship quality domains were measured along continuous five-point scales, resulting in final index ranges of 3 to 15 for each parent-adolescent attachment variable.

Dyadic parent-adolescent involvement was assessed through three activities each parent had or had not shared with his or her child in the month prior to the interview. Respondents were asked, "which of the things listed on this card have you done with your mother/father in the past 4 weeks?" and respondents answered no or yes, refused to answer, deemed the answer inapplicable, or did not know the answer. Only yes and no answers were included in the analyses. The activities, which were assessed independently for each dyadic relationship, included "gone shopping", "played a sport", and "gone to a movie, play, museum, concert, or sports event". Maternal and paternal involvement was each operationalized as an ordinal variable (0-3).

Due to the nature of the parental involvement variables, the statements produced significantly lower Cronbach's alpha coefficients than parental attachment variables. Alpha coefficients for mother-daughter, mother-son, father-daughter, and father-son involvement were .32, .29, .38, and .39, respectively. As expected, in the first interview (Wave 1), adolescents were far more likely to have gone shopping with their mothers (77.7%) than fathers (25.9%), but much less likely to have played sports with mothers (9.9%) than fathers (35.7%). However, adolescents were equally as likely to have gone to a movie, play, museum, concert, or sports event with mothers (28.8%) as fathers (28.3%). One year later, the time adolescents and parents shared together decreased. However, the trends of the prior year remained. Children shopped more often with mothers (69.8%) than fathers (23.2%), were more likely to have played sports with fathers (29.2%) than mothers (7.4%), and were equally apt to attend various events with mothers (23.2%) as fathers (23.3%).

Adolescent Developmental Age: The sample was distributed into four categories of adolescent development. The three main groups of respondents included early adolescents, or 7th and 8th graders (N=1,421); middle adolescents, or 9th and 10th graders (N=1,843); and late adolescents, consisting of 11th and 12th graders (N=1,081). The final category controlled for students who had been held back at least one grade in school to ensure that categories were age appropriate (N=720). Students who answered *yes* to the question, "have you ever repeated a grade or been held back a grade?" were designated as "held back". The category of early adolescents, defined as 7th and 8th graders, was used as the reference category. Graduated, dropped out, or suspended students as well as those out of school due pregnancy or injury were excluded from the analysis as they were not part of the school environment at the time of the interview and thus could not be appropriately lumped with other categories.

4.2.3. Supplementary Explanatory and Control Variables

Parental Educational Attainment: Maternal and paternal educational attainment were measured as ordinal variables. Each adolescent was asked to answer the question, "how far in school did your mother/father go?" by choosing from ten educational attainment choices, such as "high school graduate" or "went to college but did not graduate" (see Appendix D). Students who did not know the educational level of a parent were excluded from the analysis. Each final mother educational attainment and father educational attainment variable was then categorized into one of the following five categories: no high school diploma (reference), high school graduate or GED accredited, some post high school education but no college diploma, college graduate, or some professional training beyond college. Table 2 lists frequencies for maternal and paternal educational attainment.

Maternal Employment Status: In addition to parental education, mother's employment status was measured using mothers' parental interviews. The final mother employment status variable is measured using five categories including full-time employment, part-time employment, stay-at-home mother (unemployed and not looking for work), unemployed (unemployed and looking for work), and a final miscellaneous category including mothers who are retired, welfare recipients, or disabled. Stay-at-home mothers represent the reference category.

Adolescent Race-Ethnicity: The racial-ethnic variable was comprised of non-Hispanic White, non-Hispanic African American, Hispanic, non-Hispanic Asian, and a final category of all other ethnicities. The two questions that were used to measure race-ethnicity included "what is your race?" and "are you of Hispanic or Latino origin?" Respondents who identified with Hispanic or Latino ethnicity were categorized as Hispanic, regardless of racial identity. The majority of the sample's adolescents (65.82%) represented the reference, non-Hispanic White. In addition, immigrant status was dummy coded into two categories, immigrant or native, based on the survey question, "were you born in the United States?" The reference category, native adolescents, was compared against adolescents who were not born in the United States.

Adolescent Religiosity: Religiosity was attained using the question "how important is religion to you?" in which answer options included *very important, fairly important, fairly unimportant, not important at all,* and *no religion*. The final religion variable was comprised of three categories; very religious, fairly religious, and not religious. While very religious and fairly religious were direct representations of the first two options, the final category of not religious included those respondents who stated they had *no religion* as well as those who considered religion to be *fairly unimportant* or *not important at all*.

Sibling Composition: For the purposes of this analysis sibling composition was bracketed into five categories including adolescents with no siblings, one sibling, two siblings, three siblings, or four or more siblings. Adolescents were asked, "which child are you- the first, the second, or what?" Although respondents identified up to fifteen siblings, a dummy variable was favored since the effect of having four siblings was considered to be most similar to having five or six siblings, and due to the fact that cases per sibling group dwindled significantly beyond four siblings.

Sexual Relations: Romantic and non-romantic sexual activity, which was operationalized as a nominal variable, determined whether the respondent, at the time of the interview, was a virgin who had no sexual relations with a non-romantic partner (reference); was a virgin who had some form of sexual relations with a non-romantic partner; had sex with at least one romantic partner, but had no sexual relations with non-romantic partners; had sex with at least one romantic partner and had sexual relations with at least one non-romantic partner; had sex with a non-romantic partner, but never had sex with a romantic partner; or claimed to be a virgin but also stated to have had sex with a romantic partner. The survey asks respondents, "have you ever had sexual intercourse?" followed by a specific definition stating, "when we say sexual intercourse, we mean when a male inserts his penis into a woman's vagina". The respondent was later asked, "not counting the people you have described as romantic relationships, have you ever had a sexual relationship with anyone?" A total of five dummy categories denoting various forms of sexual experience were compared against the reference category of virgin adolescents.

Finally, whether female respondents had ever been the raped or male respondents had ever perpetrated rape was controlled for. The question asked of adolescent female respondents was, "were you ever physically forced to have sexual intercourse against your will?" while the question asked of adolescent male respondents was, "did you ever physically force someone to have sexual intercourse against her will?" Despite their differential meanings, these questions were coded as the same dichotomous variable (no=0, yes=1).

Extracurricular Participation: For the purposes of the current study, extracurricular participation included student membership in athletics or clubs. Respondents' current or planned participation in extracurricular activities for the respective school year was acquired through Wave I in-school questionnaires. First, athletic participation (e.g. hockey, field hockey) and club participation (yearbook, French, drama) were assessed separately (see Appendices D and E). The final extracurricular participation variable includes four categories: athlete only (participation in at least one sport, but no clubs), club member only (participation in at least one club, but no sports), club member and athlete (participation in at least one sport and at least one club), and neither club nor sports participant.

Quality of Friendships: To measure quality of friendships adolescents were asked, "how much do you think your friends care about you?" to which each answered, *not at all* (1), *very little* (2), *somewhat* (3), *quite a bit* (4), or *very much* (5). The final index ranges from 1 to 5 since only one question was used to assess relations with peers.

Adolescent Body Weight: In order to control for adolescent weight, adolescents' own assessments of height (feet and inches) and weight (pounds) were used to calculate a body mass index (BMI) rating. BMI was calculated as follows: [weight (lb.) ÷ height (in.)^2] X 703. The present analysis utilized the Centers for Disease Control and Prevention's BMI-for-age rating, which is designed for children and adolescents (ages 2 to 20) and is both gender and age specific. The BMI-for-age scale recognizes that specialized measurements are needed to account for the unique changes in body fat content during puberty. The Centers for Disease Control and Prevention employs the following BMI scale: Below 5th percentile (underweight), between 5th and 85th percentiles (normal weight), between 85th and 95th percentiles (at risk of overweight), and above or equal to 95th percentile (overweight). Further, BMI-for-age growth charts were used to calculate adolescent weight range categories by age and sex.

On the following page, figures 3 and 4 illustrate male and female BMI-for-age ranges used in the present analysis. The final adolescent weight variable compared respondents falling in the normal weight range (reference) against those adolescents of overweight (at or above respective 95th percentiles) and underweight (at or below 5th percentiles) ranges.

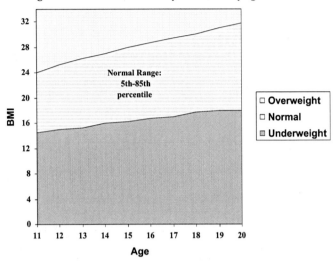

Figure 3. Female adolescent body mass index by age

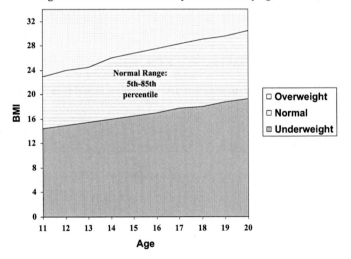

Figure 4. Male adolescent body mass index by age

4.3. Analyses

Ordinary least squares regression analyses were employed to examine the relationship between dyadic parent-adolescent relationship domains and depressed mood. Additional OLS models assessed the potential mediating effects of adolescent self-esteem as well as academic performance. All analyses utilized OLS regression models due to the continuous configuration of the depressed mood, self-esteem, and academic achievement variables. SAS statistical software was used for all analyses.

The first set of Phase I analyses, consisting of seven regression models, examined the aforementioned relationships for the entire adolescent sample. Next, the analyses were repeated, albeit separated by adolescent gender. In effect, three sets of seven models each were processed for a total of 21 regression models (refer to Tables 3-5). While the first set included the full sample of adolescents, the second examined adolescent females only, and the third focused on adolescent males only. The only difference in the variable allocation was that the first set of analyses controlled for gender.

A diagram of Phase I regression analyses is illustrated in Figure 5. As shown, within each respective set of analyses, dyadic parent-adolescent relationship domain variables were first regressed on adolescent depressed mood (Model 1). Next, all supplemental independent variables were introduced except for the self-esteem and academic achievement variables (Model 2). Adolescent self-esteem was then introduced as an explanatory variable to assess its mediating effects on adolescent depressed mood (Model 3). The following model added adolescent academic achievement to the list of explanatory variables to assess its potential mediation (Model 4). In Model 5, parental

Figure 5. Diagram of Phase I Cross-Sectional Regression Models: *Parent-Adolescent Relationships & Adolescent Depressed Mood with Mediating Variables, Self-Esteem and Academic Achievement.*

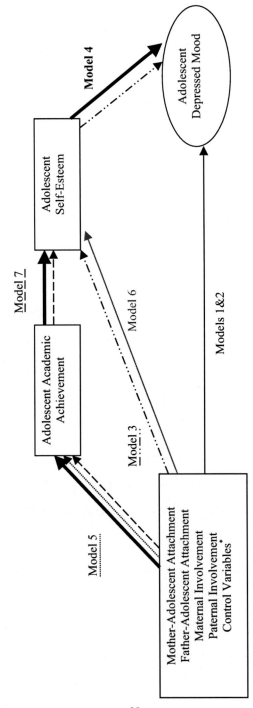

* Model 1 does not include control variables
+ Set 1 (full sample), Set 2 (females only), Set 3 (males only)

relationship and control variables were regressed on academic performance to determine its role as an outcome. Model 6 set adolescent self-esteem as the sole outcome variable and, finally, Model 7 introduced academic achievement as an explanatory variable to determine the extent to which grade point average influenced adolescent self-esteem.

Phase I also includes OLS interaction regressions that were implemented to interact dyadic parent-teen relationship quality domains with adolescent gender as well as adolescent developmental age. I examined interactive effects relating to depressed mood as well as self-esteem using full, female, and male samples. In order to examine the effects of adolescent gender and developmental age on the parent-child relations and psychosocial outcomes more specifically, I incorporated strength of paired correlation z-test analyses. Strength of paired correlation z-tests are discussed and presented later in the manuscript (Tables 6 and 7).

A second phase of analyses offers a year-long longitudinal perspective. Each model in Phase II longitudinal regressions is computed twice, once for each gender sample (Table 8). However, full sample analyses were not processed. Longitudinal analyses examined the impact of volatility in explanatory variables on depressed mood over the course of an academic year by controlling for depressed mood at time 1 (Phase II, Model 1). In this analysis, Wave I depressed mood was entered as an explanatory variable while Wave II depressed mood was introduced as the dependent variable in order to ascertain the impact of parental relations, self-esteem, and academic achievement on depressed mood over time. Likewise, the relationship between all explanatory variables was regressed on self-esteem at time 2 (Phase II, Model 2). Additional analyses longitudinally examined each dyadic parent-child relationship domain. First, time 2 mother-adolescent attachment was introduced as the sole dependent variable (Phase II, Model 3). All Wave I variables, including mother-adolescent attachment, depressed mood, self-esteem and academic achievement, were regressed on time 2 mother-teen attachment. Next, time 2 father-teen attachment was introduced (Model 4), followed by each dyadic parent-adolescent involvement variable (Models 5-6). In sum, a total of twelve regression analyses were computed in Phase II longitudinal analyses.

CHAPTER FIVE
RESULTS

5.1. Descriptive Statistics

5.1.1. T-Tests of Gender Differences: Table 1 exhibits means, standard deviations, bivariate correlations, and difference of means t-tests for applicable adolescent male and female variables. Bivariate zero-order correlation computations demonstrate that parent-adolescent relationship attachment and parental involvement variables were significantly correlated with adolescent depressed mood, self-esteem, and academic achievement in all four dyadic pairings and within both relationship domains ($p<.0001$). All 24 respective correlations showed a beneficial association by linking higher quality parent-adolescent relationships with positive emotional and scholastic outcomes. Not surprisingly, all parent-child relationship components were found to intercorrelate significantly. Outcome and mediating variables correlated significantly as well.

Table 1 also illustrates significant gender discrepancies between variables. For example, academic achievement produced slightly stronger correlations with both emotional states as it pertained to adolescent females as compared to adolescent males. Male and female teens' perceived quality of friendships were found to be significantly correlated with adolescent depressed mood, self-esteem, and dyadic parent-teen attachment ($p<.0001$). However, friendship quality was more powerfully associated with academic achievement and parental involvement for females than for males. Both boys and girls rated closer attachment and more involved relationships with mothers than with fathers. In fact, the only bivariate pairing that failed to show significance was that of

Table 1. Means, standard deviations, and zero-order correlations among continuous variables and t-tests of gender differences.

	Female Adolescents (N=2,625)								Male Adolescents (N=2,440)								T-Test
Variable (Time 1)	Mean (SD)	1	2	3	4	5	6	7	Mean (SD)	1	2	3	4	5	6	7	(t)
1. Depressed Mood (19-76)	29.68 (7.48)								28.19 (6.25)								-7.68***
2. Self-Esteem (5-30)	24.42 (3.56)	-.508***							25.52 (3.24)	-.499***							11.42***
3. Academic Achievement (1-4)	3.06 (.716)	-.272***	.199***						2.84 (.761)	-.227***	.144***						-10.45***
4. Mother-Child Attachment (3-15)	13.80 (1.62)	-.322***	.398***	.156***					14.11 (1.20)	-.239***	.365***	.086***					7.69***
5. Father-Child Attachment (3-15)	13.25 (2.03)	-.322***	.385***	.194***	.456***				13.66 (1.65)	-.308***	.394***	.101***	.470***				7.72***
6. Maternal Involvement (0-3)	4.25 (.740)	-.198***	.148***	.140***	.234***	.189***			4.08 (.784)	-.143***	.172***	.151***	.168***	.171***			-8.08***
7. Paternal Involvement (0-3)	3.76 (.873)	-.181***	.171***	.161***	.156***	.311***	.450***		4.04 (.952)	-.159***	.159***	.178***	.131***	.257***	.501***		10.98***
8. Quality of Friendships (0-5)	4.44 (.690)	-.177***	.206***	.090***	.177***	.187***	.062**	.055**	4.16 (.764)	-.225***	.259***	.077***	.161***	.172***	.041*	.036	-13.76***

Levels of significance: *p<.05, **p<.01, ***p<.0001

friendship quality and father-son involvement.

T-tests exhibited clear gender differences in adolescents' emotional and cognitive well-being. On average, boys fared better emotionally than girls as is demonstrated in results showing significantly higher mean levels of self-esteem ($p<.0001$) and lower mean levels of depressed mood ($p<.0001$) among adolescent boys compared to girls (refer to Table 1). On the other hand, the present sample's adolescent girls outperformed adolescent boys scholastically ($p<.0001$), exhibiting a considerably higher mean grade point average (3.06) than boys (2.84). According to t-test analyses, boys perceived stronger attachment to both parental figures and assessed significantly greater involvement from fathers than did girls ($p<.0001$). However, girls' perceptions of maternal involvement were significantly higher than boys' estimates ($p<.0001$). Finally, adolescent females believed they had significantly higher quality friendships than did adolescent males ($p<.0001$).

5.1.2. Frequencies: Table 2 displays frequencies for nominal and ordinal variables. As shown, mothers and fathers had similar levels of educational attainment. The mode for each parent was having had received a high school diploma, but no additional education. Representative of national estimates, the majority of mothers in the sample worked fulltime (53.4%) while mothers employed part-time (18.8%) and stay-at-home mothers (17.3%) represented the next most common types of employment status. The majority of respondents resided with one (42.7%) or two (30.2%) other siblings while only 11.1% of the sample were only children.

Developmental ages were fairly evenly distributed, although most respondents

Table 2. Frequencies for ordinal and nominal variables N(%).

	Parental Educational Attainment					
Sample (Full)	No High School	High School Graduate	Post High School	College Graduate	Post College	Total
Mother	655 (12.93)	1,743 (34.41)	953 (18.82)	1,217 (24.03)	497 (9.81)	5,065 (100)
Father	731 (14.43)	1,526 (30.13)	939 (18.54)	1,187 (23.44)	682 (13.46)	5,065 (100)

	Maternal Employment Status					
Sample	Stay-at-Home	Full-time	Part-time	Unemployed	Retired, Disabled Welfare Recipient	Total
Full	874 (17.26)	2,702 (53.35)	954 (18.84)	179 (3.53)	356 (7.03)	5,065 (100)

	Sibling Composition					
Sample	Only Child	1 Sibling	2 Siblings	3 Siblings	4 Siblings	Total
Full	563 (11.12)	2,160 (42.65)	1,529 (30.19)	564 (11.14)	249 (4.92)	5,065 (100)

	Race-Ethnicity					
Sample	Non-Hispanic White	Non-Hispanic Black	Hispanic	Non-Hispanic Asian	Other	Total
Full	3,334 (65.82)	630 (12.44)	735 (14.51)	305 (6.02)	61 (1.20)	5,065 (100)

	School Grade					
Sample	Early Adolescence (7-8th Grade)	Mid Adolescence (9-10th Grade)	Late Adolescence (11-12th Grade)	Held Back		Total
Full	1,421 (28.06)	1,843 (36.39)	1,081 (21.34)	720 (14.22)		5,065 (100)

	Religiosity					
Sample		Not Religious	Fairly Religious	Very Religious		Total
Females		427 (16.27)	927 (35.31)	1,271 (48.42)		2,625 (51.83)
Males						2,440 (48.17)

	Body Weight: BMI Index Range					
Sample		Underweight	Normal	Overweight		Total
Females		67 (2.55)	2,368 (90.21)	190 (7.24)		2,625 (51.83)
Males		68 (2.79)	2,065 (84.63)	307 (12.58)		2,440 (48.17)

	School Extracurricular Participation					
Sample		Neither Club Nor Athlete	School Club Only	Athlete Only	Both Club Member And Athlete	Total
Females		912 (34.74)	588 (22.40)	211 (8.04)	914 (34.82)	2,625 (51.83)
Males		927 (37.99)	241 (9.88)	621 (25.45)	651 (26.68)	2,440 (48.17)

	Sexual Experience[1]					
Sample	Virgin	Virgin, Had Casual Relations	Romantic Sex, No Casual Relations	Casual Sex Only	Casual and Romantic Sex	Claims Virginity, Had Romantic Sex
Females	1,956 (74.51)	48 (1.83)	244 (9.30)	75 (2.86)	225 (8.57)	77 (2.93)
Males	1,675 (68.65)	124 (5.08)	173 (7.09)	137 (5.61)	231 (9.47)	100 (4.10)

[1] total 2,625 females; 2,440 males

were mid-adolescents at the time of the survey (36.4%). 65.8% of the sample was non-Hispanic White and 48.4% of adolescents considered themselves *very religious*. A clear majority of adolescents fell within the normal body mass index range (90.2% of females and 84.6% of males). Although comparable numbers of girls were neither club nor sports participants (34.7%) as were both club and athletic members (34.8%), most boys fell within the former category (38%). The major gender difference in extracurricular participation was that females were nearly two and one-half times more likely than males to be just club members while males were nearly three times more likely to have athletic status only (refer to Table 2). A substantial majority of adolescents were virgins at the time of the interview (74.5% of females and 68.7% of males) while cases in the remaining five categories of sexual experience were, for the most part, dispersed.

5.2. Full Sample Cross-Sectional Regression Analyses

As discussed previously, ordinary least squares regression analyses were performed to analyze the relationship between dyadic parent-child relationship quality and adolescent depressed mood. All seven full sample cross-sectional regressions, presented in Table 3, were significant at p<.0001 levels.

5.2.1. Baseline Regressions (Models I and II): Model I (R^2=.147), which regresses parent-adolescent relationship domains on adolescent depressed mood, demonstrates that females tended to have significantly higher depressive symptomatology than the reference category, adolescent males (p<.0001, b=.936). Dyadic parent-teen attachment and maternal involvement were significantly and inversely related to adolescent depressed mood (p<.0001) as was paternal involvement, albeit to a slightly lesser degree (p<.01).

Model II expanded the first model to include control variables and explained a total of 21.2% of the variance in adolescent depressed mood. The controls impacted parental involvement such that, from Model I to Model II, the association between maternal involvement and adolescent depressed mood diminished in significance (p<.01) as well as correlative effect (-35%) while paternal involvement lost significance altogether. Compared to mothers with no high school education, having a mother with higher educational attainment was associated with lower rates of adolescent depressed mood (p<.01- p<.0001). Although higher paternal education was also inversely associated with depressed mood, results are less consistent (refer to Table 3). Compared to adolescents with stay-at-home mothers, youth with mothers who worked fulltime (p<.05) or had mothers who were unemployed, retired, disabled, or on welfare (p<.10) were more likely to be depressed.

Overall, adolescents tended to become more depressed at each developmental age as indicated by increasing developmental association of mid-adolescent (p<.10, b=.433) and late adolescent (p<.01, b=.859) dummies compared to the early adolescent reference category. In addition, respondents who had been held back a grade were at significantly greater risk for depressed mood than early adolescents (p<.0001, b=1.46). While non-Hispanic Black adolescents did not show significant differences in risks for depression as compared to White adolescents, both Hispanic (p<.01) and Asian (p<.0001) adolescents tended to be more depressed than Caucasian peers. Depressed mood appeared to be particularly problematic for Asian respondents, who were over three times more likely

TABLE 3. Full sample ordinary least squares regression models of dyadic parent-adolescent relationship quality on adolescent depressed mood, self-esteem and GPA (N=5,065).

Variable [reference]	Model I Depressed Mood		Model II Depressed Mood		Model III Depressed Mood		Model IV Depressed Mood		Model V GPA		Model VI Self-Esteem		Model VII Self-Esteem	
	b	SD	b	SD	b	SD	b	SD	b	SD	b	SD	b	SD
Primary														
Gender (0=male, 1=female)	.936***	.188	1.49***	.197	.614**	.183	.773***	.184	.155***	.021	-1.06***	.094	-1.13***	.094
Relations with Parents														
Mother-Adolescent Attachment	-.831***	.072	-.748***	.070	-.292***	.066	-.281***	.066	.024***	.007	.546***	.030	.535***	.033
Father-Adolescent Attachment	-.781***	.057	-.632***	.056	-.290***	.053	-.283***	.052	.018**	.006	.410***	.027	.401***	.026
Maternal Involvement	-.689***	.137	-.450**	.134	-.318*	.123	-.295*	.122	.028*	.014	.158*	.063	.146*	.063
Paternal Involvement	-.373**	.116	-.107	.104	.003	.105	.033	.105	.035**	.012	.131*	.054	.113*	.054
Mediating														
Self-Esteem					-.835***	.027	-.814***	.027						
Academic Achievement							-.937***	.123					.469***	.064
Controls														
Mother's Education [no high school]														
High School			-1.25***	.327	-.963**	.300	-.931**	.298	.042	.034	.336*	.155	.316*	.154
Post High School			-1.20***	.364	-.869*	.335	-.779*	.333	.106**	.038	.382*	.173	.332*	.172
College Graduate			-1.26***	.376	-1.24***	.345	-1.06**	.344	.183***	.040	.016	.178	-.070	.178
Post College			-1.53***	.465	-1.30**	.427	-1.05*	.426	.279***	.049	.258	.221	.127	.220
Father's Education [no high school]														
High School			-.385	.314	-.663*	.289	-.640*	.287	.023	.033	-.333***	.155	-.343*	.148
Post High School			-.930**	.347	-1.12**	.389	-.997**	.317	.123**	.037	-.224	.173	-.273+	.164
College Graduate			-1.14**	.354	-1.27***	.325	-1.10**	.324	.177***	.037	-.151	.178	-.229	.168
Post College			-.702*	.414	-.833*	.380	-.610	.379	.235***	.044	-.157	.221	-.259	.196
Mother's Employment [stay-at-home]														
Fulltime			.523*	.250	.598*	.230	.591*	.228	-.009	.026	.091	.026	.095	.118
Parttime			.419	.293	.454+	.269	.475*	.268	.024	.031	.041	.031	.030	.139
Unemployed			.983*	.514	1.01*	.472	.990*	.470	-.031	.054	.027	.054	.042	.243
Retired, Welfare, Disabled			.654*	.398	.783*	.365	.773*	.363	.006	.042	.154	.042	.151	.188
Developmental Age [Early Adolescence- 7-8th]														
Middle Adolescence (9-10th Grade)			.433+	.226	.009	.208	-.074	.207	-.082***	.024	-.530***	.108	-.492***	.107
Late Adolescence (11-12th Grade)			.859***	.270	.315	.249	.299	.247	.032	.028	-.653***	.128	-.638***	.128
Held Back			1.46***	.306	1.11***	.281	.793**	.283	-.347***	.032	-.426**	.145	-.263+	.146

Levels of significance: +p<.10, *p<.05, **p<.01, ***p<.0001

97

TABLE 3. Continued.

Variable [reference]	Model I b	Model I SD	Model II b	Model II SD	Model III b	Model III SD	Model IV b	Model IV SD	Model V b	Model V SD	Model VI b	Model VI SD	Model VII b	Model VII SD
Race-Ethnicity [non-Hispanic White]														
Non-Hispanic Black			.072	.286	.960**	.264	.713**	.265	-.241***	.030	1.06***	.136	1.17***	.136
Hispanic			.754**	.284	.724**	.261	.581*	.260	-.155***	.030	-.036	.135	.036	.135
Non-Hispanic Asian			2.45***	.382	2.06***	.351	2.15***	.349	.080*	.040	-.467**	.181	-.497**	.181
Other			.124	.808	.610	.742	.470	.738	-.139	.085	.581†	.384	.645†	.382
Immigrant Status [native]														
Immigrant			-.162	.200	-.146	.184	-.171	.183	-.026	.021	.019	.095	.031	.095
Religiosity [not religious]														
Fairly Religious			.103	.253	.141	.232	.173	.232	.037	.027	.045	.120	.028	.119
Very Religious			.155	.252	.391†	.232	.500*	.231	.128***	.026	.277*	.120	.216†	.119
Sibling Composition [only child]														
1 Sibling			.252	.296	.308	.271	.304	.270	.016	.031	.053	.141	.045	.140
2 Siblings			.634*	.309	.593*	.284	.589*	.283	.029	.033	-.070	.147	-.084	.147
3 Siblings			.626*	.375	.630*	.345	.567	.344	-.030	.040	.018	.179	-.004	.178
4+ Siblings			.326	.483	.593	.443	.559	.442	.009	.051	.301	.230	.306	.228
Sexual Experience [virgin]														
Virgin, nonromantic relations			1.54***	.490	1.17**	.450	.930*	.448	-.269***	.055	-.434†	.232	-.308	.232
Romantic sex, no nonromantic relations			1.11**	.337	1.20***	.310	1.06***	.308	-.137***	.035	.107	.160	.172	.159
Nonromantic sex only			1.19**	.457	1.41**	.420	1.10**	.420	-.287***	.048	.248	.218	.338†	.217
Romantic sex and nonromantic relations			1.81***	.331	1.93***	.304	1.61***	.301	-.304***	.035	.132	.158	.275*	.158
Claims virginity, had romantic sex			.650	.489	.617	.449	.426	.447	-.189**	.051	-.040	.232	.049	.231
Forced Sexual Experience [never raped]														
Rape Victim (female), Rapist (male)			1.39*	.627	1.29*	.576	1.37*	.573	.065	.066	-.094	.298	-.125	.296
Extracurricular Participation [neither]														
School Club			-.413	.266	-.363	.245	-.230	.244	.145***	.030	.060	.127	-.008	.126
School Athletics			-.628*	.266	-.463†	.245	-.487*	.243	-.012	.028	.197	.126	.203	.126
Both Club and Athletics			-.652**	.222	-.374†	.204	.203	.204	.191***	.023	.333**	.105	.243*	.106
Relations with Peers														
Quality of Friendships			-1.10***	.125	-.493***	.116	-.500***	.115	.006	.013	.731***	.059	.728***	.059
Body Weight [normal BMI range]														
Overweight			.750*	.300	.164	.275	.080	.274	-.104**	.031	-.701***	.142	-.647***	.141
Underweight			.626	.546	.548	.501	.528	.498	-.024	.057	-.093	.259	-.082	.258
Intercept	54.89***	.989	54.26***	1.21	61.03***	1.13	62.63***	1.14	1.88***	.127	7.95***	.564	7.07***	.574
R²	.147		.212		.335		.343		.244		.277		.285	

Levels of significance: †p<.10, *p<.05, **p<.01, ***p<.0001

than White youth to be depressed.

Although sibling effects were relatively inconsistent, they nonetheless indicated that adolescents with two or three siblings were at greater risk for depressive symptoms than peers who were only children (p<.05- p<.01). In general, sexually experienced adolescents were more depressed than virgins. As a whole, respondents who reported to have had sex, either romantic or nonromantic sexual relations, were at greater risk for depression. Experience with rape, whether female adolescents who responded that they had been raped or male adolescents who claimed to have perpetrated rape, were more depressed than those respondents who had never been involved in rape (p<.05). Compared to students who were not engaged in extracurricular activities, members of athletic teams (p<.05) as well as participants in both clubs and sports (p<.01) were less likely to be depressed. Club membership alone was not associated with depressive state. On average, quality of friendships were inversely associated with depressed mood (p<.0001) while overweight (but not underweight) adolescents were more likely to internalize mood disturbance than peers of the normal weight range (p<.05).

5.2.2. Mediation Regressions (Models III and IV): Model III initiated the examination of mediation by introducing adolescent self-esteem as an explanatory variable. Self-esteem raised the R-square from .212 to .335, signifying a copious increase in variance explained by the model. Self-esteem was highly significant and inversely associated with depressed mood (p<.0001). The association between gender and depressive symptomatology was greatly reduced with the inclusion of self-esteem. While adolescent females were still more likely to be depressed than adolescent males, the association was less significant (p<.01) and the coefficient decreased by nearly 60% (see Table 3, Model III). Similarly, the negative coefficient for mother-adolescent attachment, linking stronger attachment with lower depressive affect, decreased by over 60% while self-esteem attenuated the correlative power of father-adolescent attachment by one-half. In spite of this, parental involvement was only moderately impacted by the addition of self-esteem.

While the inverse association between maternal education and depressive affect was weakened in Model III, the relationship of both paternal education and maternal employment, with corresponding lesser and greater depressed mood, became somewhat stronger.

The association between developmental age and depressed mood disappeared as a result of self-esteem's attenuation, although being held back only lost one-quarter of its correlative strength. Results associated with race were uniquely transformed from Model I to Model III. Compared to being non-Hispanic White, being non-Hispanic Black materialized as significantly associated with lower depressive affect (p<.01) while the coefficient linking Asian adolescents with increased depressive symptoms decreased by 15%. However, the relationship between Hispanic ethnicity and depressed mood remained unchanged. Considering oneself very religious, as compared to not religious at all, emerged as a fairly significant variable (p<.10). Association was positive, linking increased religiosity with greater mood disturbance. Sibling composition, sexual experience, and connection with rape showed no clear or significant transformation. The prior significance of athletic or both athletic and club membership, as compared to neither status in protecting adolescents from depressive affect were both lessened by the insertion of self-esteem (p<.10). In addition to lower levels of significance, the sports participation coefficient lost over one-quarter of its power while dual participation was diminished by roughly 40%. In Model III, the significance of overweight status (compared to normal) vanished entirely, thus signifying full mediation.

In Model IV I incorporated further mediation by adding adolescent academic achievement, based on adolescent grade point average, to the regression. Although GPA was found to be highly and inversely related to depressed mood (p<.0001), it only increased the R-square by .008, or roughly 2 percent. Supplementing academic performance to the regression amplified the significance (p<.0001) and correlation (+25.9%) of the gender dummy variable. Although attachment relationships were not significantly affected by GPA's entry, maternal involvement became less significant (p<.05) to adolescent depression (b= -.295).

In general, the strong relationship that existed between increased parental education and lower depressive symptoms in the prior model were diluted considerably in Model IV. Moreover, resultant loss of significance and decreased coefficients indicated that mediation effects became more significant as parental educational attainment increased. For example, while mothers' and fathers' high school education dummies lost only minimal strength (-5%), the coefficient for the highest educational attainment category, post college education, decreased by 20% (mothers) and 27% (fathers). In fact, post college educated fathers became insignificant to depressive state once GPA was accounted for. Likewise, the effect of having a fully employed mother, compared to a stay-at-home mother, became less significant to depressive outcomes (p<.05).

Held back adolescents represented the sole remaining developmental age category to still exhibit significance once GPA was accounted for. Although held back adolescents continued to be more depressed than early adolescents, adolescent school performance attenuated some effect of being held back on self-esteem ($p<.01$, 30% coefficient reduction). Both racial-ethnic categories of non-Hispanic Black and Hispanic were not as powerfully associated with the dependent variable once GPA was introduced. The coefficient associated with African American status lost one-quarter of its strength while the Hispanic dummy variable lost one-fifth of its strength and became less significant to depressed mood ($p<.01$).

As a whole, the prior significance linking additional siblings, non-virgin status, and dual extracurricular participation with higher risk for depression were all weakened by the introduction of scholastic performance. In contrast, the significant inverse association between being an athlete and depressed mood as well as the positive association of high religiosity and psychological disturbance were all strengthened by grade point average. Finally, the coefficients connected to the rape and friendship quality variables remained relatively unchanged from Model III to Model IV.

5.2.3. Academic Achievement and Self-Esteem Regressions (Models V, VI, and VII):
Model V replaced the dependent variable, depressed mood, with academic achievement (grade point average). With the exception of adolescent self-esteem and GPA, I utilized the same explanatory variables as in the previous model. The entire model explained 24.4% of the variance in academic achievement. Corroborating t-test analyses, adolescent females were shown to have significantly higher grades than adolescent males

(p<.0001). Parent-child attachment and paternal involvement were positively associated with GPA at p<.01 levels while maternal involvement was slightly less significant at p<.05. For the most part, increased educational attainment among both mothers and fathers was similarly related to higher adolescent grades (see Model V). However, maternal employment failed to show significance.

On average, middle adolescents (p<.01, $b=-.082$) and particularly those respondents held back in school (p<.001, $b=-.347$) had lower GPAs than early adolescents. Regressions demonstrated that White adolescents had nearly two and one-half times better grade point averages than African American adolescents and over one and one-half times better grade point averages than Hispanics (p<.0001). In contrast, Asian students tended to perform slightly better academically than White students (p<.05, $b=.080$). Students who considered themselves to be very religious had significantly higher school grades than those adolescents who stated they were not religious at all (p<.0001). According to Model V regressions, sexually experienced adolescents fared considerably worse in the classroom than virgin counterparts. Youth who reported to have had romantic sex and nonromantic sexual relations had, on average, the poorest grades (refer to Model V). Being a member of a school club or both sport team and club, compared to having no extracurricular involvement at all, was positively associated with academic achievement (p<.0001). The current sample's overweight adolescents were found to have lower grades than adolescents of normal weight (p<.01). Sibling composition, experience with rape, and quality of friendships were not found to be associated with adolescent scholastic performance.

The final two models of the full sample analyses set adolescent self-esteem as the dependent variable. Model VI, which did not include academic achievement, explained 27.7% of the variance in adolescent self-esteem. Adolescent girls suffered considerably lower self-esteem than boys ($p<.0001$, $b= -1.06$). Parental attachment, particularly maternal attachment, as well as parental involvement, particularly paternal involvement, were significantly related to adolescent self-esteem at the $p<.0001$ and $p<.05$ levels, respectively. Despite its lack of statistical consistency, mother's education revealed some positive association while father's education showed some inverse association with adolescent self-esteem (refer to Model VI).

Taken as a whole, adolescents' self-esteem levels tended to decline with developmental age ($p<.0001$) and when held back in school ($p<.01$). Analyses showed that Black adolescents had significantly higher self-esteem than White adolescents ($p<.0001$), but Asian teens, on average, had half the self-esteem levels as White peers ($p<.01$). Compared to no extracurricular involvement, only dual club and athletics participation was associated with higher self-esteem ($p<.05$). Respondents' perceptions of friendship quality were significantly associated with higher self-esteem ($p<.0001$) while being overweight was significantly associated with decreased self-esteem ($p<.0001$). Maternal employment, sibling composition, and sexual experiences were not found to be related to adolescent self-esteem in Model VI.

Next, the academic performance variable was introduced in the Model VII analysis. Although the addition only resulted in a .008 overall increase in variance explained by the model, adolescent grade point average was nonetheless significantly and positively related to self-esteem ($p<.0001$). As a whole, academic achievement did not materialize as a significant mediator to the majority of variables in the regression. Although GPA failed to significantly mediate parental attachment relationships, it did impact the relationship between parental involvement and self-esteem. Although the coefficient associated with maternal involvement was only minimally mediated by GPA, the paternal involvement coefficient decreased by 15% in Model VII. Mediation effects slightly weakened significant maternal education, developmental age, religiosity, dual extracurricular involvement status, and body weight variable coefficients. Matched up against the White peers, the positive association between African American status and self-esteem as well as the negative association between Asian American status and self-esteem remained relatively unchanged despite the insertion of grade point average.

5.2.4. Synopsis of Primary Variable Effects: Adolescent gender was found to be strongly associated with adolescents' emotional and cognitive outcomes. As expected, girls were significantly more likely to be depressed than boys. However, the insertion of the self-esteem mediator substantially weakened the relationship even though girls, on average, still faced significantly greater depressive risks than boys. From Model II to Model III, the gender variable became less significant ($p<.01$) and the strength of its coefficient decreased by over 60%. In corroboration of bivariate correlations and t-tests (Table 1), being an adolescent female as opposed to an adolescent male was positively and significantly associated with higher academic achievement and lower self-esteem ($p<.0001$).

Overall, teen attachment to both mothers and fathers were similarly and significantly related to adolescent depressed mood ($p<.0001$). Although variables retained prior levels of significance, mother and father attachment dyads were strongly mediated by adolescent self-esteem. Not surprisingly, Model VI, in which self-esteem represented the outcome, showed both attachment relationships to be positively associated with adolescent self-esteem ($p<.0001$). Although parent-adolescent attachment relations were also significant, and equally so, to academic achievement ($p<.01$) in Model V, GPA failed to notably mediate the relationship between parental attachment and depressed mood in Model IV.

Attachment relations, regardless of parent or adolescent gender, were found to be more significant to child well-being than parental involvement relationships. In fact, only maternal involvement remained significant once the controls were inserted in Model II ($p<.01$). Self-esteem partially attenuated the influence of maternal involvement, although not to the extent in which it had mediated parental attachment (Model III). GPA, on the other hand, emerged as a stronger mediator in the relationship between maternal involvement and depressed mood than parental attachment and depressed mood (Model IV). Although Model V, in which explanatory variables were regressed on GPA, displayed both involvement relationships to be significant to adolescent academic achievement, involvement of fathers ($p<.01$) was more significant to the outcome variable than maternal involvement ($p<.05$). Similarly, the correlative power of father-child involvement to adolescent self-esteem was over twice as strong as mother-child involvement (Model VI). In the final model, GPA proved to partially, albeit minimally, mediate the preceding relationships between parental involvement and self-esteem (Model VII).

5.3. Female and Male Cross-Sectional Regression Analyses

Tables 4 and 5 illustrate regression results for corresponding female and male samples. All fourteen cross-sectional models were significant at the .0001 levels and explained up to 34.8% and 33.7% of the variance in female and male depressed mood, respectively.

5.3.1. Baseline Regressions (Models I and II): Model I regressions, which explained 15.6% (female) and 11.5% (male) of the variance in adolescent depressed mood, displayed significant and inverse association among all dyadic parent-adolescent relationship domains. While all four dyadic attachment relationships achieved significance at p<.0001 levels, comparing coefficients revealed that attachment to same-sex parents was more salient to adolescent psychological health than cross-sex attachment. The coefficient associated with mother-daughter attachment was strongest (-.936) followed by father-son attachment (-.872), father-daughter attachment (-.728), and mother-son attachment (-.596). As illustrated in Table 4, Model I, perceptions of maternal involvement were powerfully linked to female depressed mood (p<.0001, b= -.932) although paternal involvement produced significant association as well (p<.05, b= -.398). Although parental involvement and adolescent male depressed mood were also related to male depressive symptomatology (p<.05), it was actually maternal involvement that exhibited a slightly greater coefficient (-.446) than paternal involvement (-.371).

Incorporating controls strengthened the models, as is seen in new estimated R-squares of roughly .21 for both models. While none of the attachment variables changed notably, all four parental involvement variables were weakened. In fact, maternal involvement within the female sample was the only involvement variable to retain any significance at all (p<.01, *b*= -.622). In regard to dyadic parent-adolescent relationship domains, regressions continued to maintain that same-sex attachment, but more specifically that of mothers and daughters, produced the most powerful correlation with depressed mood (.860).

Despite the fact that results associated with parental educational attainment were generally inconsistent, they did suggest that increased parental education was related to lower risk for depression among teens. Overall, maternal education was more salient to both male and female adolescent depressed mood than was paternal education (refer to Tables 4 and 5, Model II). Compared to having mothers who were homemakers, girls whose mothers were employed or unemployed, but looking for work were only marginally more likely to be depressed (p<.10). Maternal employment was insignificant in the male sample model.

Overall, adolescent developmental age was determined to be most significant to male psychological state (see Table 5). According to the regressions, boys became increasingly depressed with each stage of adolescence (p<.0001) while girls were only shown to be significantly more depressed during mid-adolescence as compared to early adolescence (p<.05). Although having been held back in school had negative repercussions for teenagers' emotional well-being, boys were most negatively impacted overall (refer to Table 5, Model II).

Racial-ethnic findings emphasized Asian students' susceptibility to depression. Both male and female Asian youth were over two times more likely to suffer depressive affect than White peers (p<.0001). Hispanic males were also more likely to be depressed

TABLE 4. Female sample ordinary least squares regression models of dyadic parent-adolescent relationship quality on adolescent depressed mood, self-esteem and GPA (N=2,625).

Variable [reference]	Model I Depressed Mood		Model II Depressed Mood		Model III Depressed Mood		Model IV Depressed Mood		Model V GPA		Model VI Self-Esteem		Model VII Self-Esteem	
	b	SD	b	SD	b	SD	b	SD	b	SD	b	SD	b	SD
Primary														
Relations with Parents														
Mother-Daughter Attachment	-.936***	.095	-.860***	.094	-.373***	.089	-.364***	.089	.021*	.009	.555***	.043	.544***	.043
Father-Daughter Attachment	-.728***	.077	-.547***	.078	-.215**	.073	-.196**	.072	.026**	.007	.378***	.035	.365***	.036
Maternal Involvement	-.932***	.207	-.662**	.205	-.587**	.188	-.559**	.186	.026	.019	.089	.094	.072	.094
Paternal Involvement	-.398*	.179	-.158	.178	-.036	.163	-.024	.162	.014	.017	.144+	.082	.132+	.081
Mediating														
Self-Esteem					-.876***	.039	-.849***	.039						
Academic Achievement							-1.18***	.191					.545***	.095
Controls														
Mother's Education [no high school]														
High School			-1.28**	.484	-1.14*	.443	-1.10*	.440	.028	.045	.155	.222	.147	.221
Post High School			-.979+	.535	-.692	.489	-.549	.486	.116*	.050	.333	.245	.281	.244
College Graduate			-1.45**	.560	-1.38**	.512	-1.33**	.511	.213***	.053	.089	.257	-.011	.256
Post College			-1.82**	.693	-1.63*	.634	-1.33*	.632	.234***	.065	.219	.318	.019	.317
Father's Education [no high school]														
High School			-.411	.465	-.778+	.426	-.698	.424	.058	.044	-.413+	.214	-.445*	.212
Post High School			-1.06*	.514	-1.25**	.470	-1.03*	.468	.177***	.048	-.211	.236	-.311	.235
College Graduate			-1.15*	.527	-1.21*	.482	-.990*	.480	.186***	.050	-.063	.242	-.173	.241
Post College			-.665	.613	-.854	.561	-.565	.559	.240***	.058	-.202	.281	-.345	.281
Mother's Employment [stay-at-home]														
Fulltime			.697+	.373	.824*	.342	.844*	.339	.018	.035	.139	.171	.129	.170
Parttime			.821+	.445	.727+	.408	.790+	.405	.050	.042	-.111	.204	-.138	.203
Unemployed			1.41+	.774	1.63*	.709	1.78*	.704	.131+	.073	.218	.356	.147	.354
Retired, Welfare, Disabled			.881	.592	1.20*	.542	1.21*	.538	.021	.056	.349	.272	.343	.270
Developmental Age [Early Adolescence- 7-8th]														
Middle Adolescence (9-10th Grade)			.773*	.336	.292	.308	.172	.306	-.114***	.032	-.549***	.154	-.487***	.154
Late Adolescence (11-12th Grade)			.208	.401	-.232	.367	-.279	.365	-.051	.038	-.502**	.184	-.474**	.183
Held Back			1.23*	.497	.701	.456	.323	.457	-.334***	.047	-.598**	.228	-.416+	.229

Levels of significance: +p<.10, *p<.05, **p<.01, ***p<.0001

TABLE 4. Continued.

Variable [reference]	Model I b	Model I SD	Model II b	Model II SD	Model III b	Model III SD	Model IV b	Model IV SD	Model V b	Model V SD	Model VI b	Model VI SD	Model VII b	Model VII SD
Race-Ethnicity [non-Hispanic White]														
Non-Hispanic Black			.390	.415	1.49***	.383	1.16**	.383	-.225***	.039	1.25***	.190	1.35***	.190
Hispanic			.652	.428	.745⁺	.392	.446	.390	-.222***	.040	.095	.196	.192	.196
Non-Hispanic Asian			2.62***	.614	2.20***	.562	2.36***	.558	.123*	.058	-.477⁺	.281	-.546	.280
Other			.087	1.39	1.07	1.27	.939	1.26	-.066	.131	1.12*	.638	1.13⁺	.634
Immigrant Status [native]														
Immigrant			-.383	.300	-.280	.275	-.299	.273	-.013	.028	.117	.138	.124	.137
Religiosity [not religious]														
Fairly Religious			.321	.398	.314	.364	.409	.362	.081*	.037	-.009	.183	-.052	.183
Very Religious			.199	.392	.573	.359	.780*	.357	.181***	.037	.434*	.180	.335*	.179
Sibling Composition [only child]														
1 Sibling			.072	.463	-.013	.423	.004	.421	.046	.043	-.097	.212	-.122	.211
2 Siblings			.678	.486	.449	.445	.536	.442	.068	.046	-.261	.223	-.298	.222
3 Siblings			.774	.574	.467	.525	.497	.522	.016	.054	-.349	.263	-.358	.262
4+ Siblings			.743	.729	.637	.667	.670	.663	.025	.069	-.121	.334	-.134	.332
Sexual Experience [virgin]														
Virgin, nonromantic relations			2.48*	.991	1.65*	.908	1.28*	.903	-.331***	.093	-.953*	.454	-.773⁺	.453
Romantic sex, no nonromantic relations			1.65***	.485	1.88***	.445	1.71***	.442	-.136**	.046	.268	.223	.342	.222
Nonromantic sex only			.579	.837	.850	.766	.343	.765	-.422***	.079	.309	.384	.384	.384
Romantic sex and nonromantic relations			2.29***	.520	2.38***	.476	2.02***	.474	-.287***	.049	-.095	.238	.251	.239
Claims virginity, had romantic sex			.758	.806	.844	.738	.583	.734	-.219**	.076	-.098	.370	.217	.368
Forced Sexual Experience [never raped]														
Rape Victim			1.62*	.754	1.32*	.691	1.40*	.685	.064	.071	-.341	.346	-.376	.344
Extracurricular Participation [neither]														
School Club			-.288	.361	-.296	.331	-.182	.329	.096**	.034	-.009	.166	-.060	.165
School Athletics			-.801	.520	-.242	.476	-.321	.472	-.071	.049	-.184	.238	-.146	.237
Both Club and Athletics			-.547⁺	.326	-.378	.298	-.231	.297	.128***	.031	.193	.149	.123	.149
Relations with Peers														
Quality of Friendships			-.984***	.198	-.404*	.183	-.414*	.182	.007	.019	.662***	.091	.658***	.090
Body Weight [normal BMI range]														
Overweight			.517	.516	-.318	.474	-.445	.471	-.128**	.049	-.935***	.237	-.865***	.236
Underweight			.105	.838	.408	.767	.407	.762	-.007	.079	-.345	.384	-.341	.382
Intercept	57.71***	1.32	56.49***	1.75	63.38***	1.61	65.51***	1.63	1.97***	.165	7.92***	.791	6.84***	.807
R^2	.156		.211		.339		.348		.238		.264		.273	

Levels of significance: ⁺p<.10, *p<.05, **p<.01, ***p<.0001

TABLE 5. Male sample ordinary least squares regression models of dyadic parent-adolescent relationship quality on adolescent depressed mood, self-esteem and GPA (N=2,440).

Variable [reference]	Model I Depressed Mood		Model II Depressed Mood		Model III Depressed Mood		Model IV Depressed Mood		Model V GPA		Model VI Self-Esteem		Model VII Self-Esteem	
	b	SD	b	SD	b	SD	b	SD	b	SD	b	SD	b	SD
Primary														
Relations with Parents														
Mother-Son Attachment	-.596***	.113	-.499***	.110	-.091	.103	-.082	.103	.024+	.013	.522***	.055	.513***	.054
Father-Son Attachment	-.872***	.084	-.728***	.082	-.364***	.077	-.367***	.077	.006	.010	.467***	.041	.464***	.040
Maternal Involvement	-.446*	.177	-.277	.172	-.076	.159	-.051	.158	.039*	.021	.257*	.085	.242*	.085
Paternal Involvement	-.371*	.148	-.085	.145	-.016	.133	.019	.133	.048**	.017	.088	.072	.070	.072
Mediating														
Self-Esteem					-.782***	.039	-.765***	.038						
Academic Achievement							-.747***	.157					.387***	.085
Controls														
Mother's Education [no high school]														
High School			-1.26**	.438	-.859*	.404	-.821*	.402	.062	.052	.518*	.218	.494*	.217
Post High School			-1.46**	.492	-1.08*	.454	-1.01*	.452	.099*	.590	.487*	.245	.448*	.244
College Graduate			-1.06*	.499	-.983*	.460	-.962*	.459	.154**	.060	-.022	.248	-.083	.248
Post College			-1.25*	.618	-.590*	.570	-.751+	.569	.319***	.074	.340	.307	.217	.307
Father's Education [no high school]														
High School			-.367	.419	-.590	.386	-.604	.384	-.026	.050	-.286	.208	-.276	.207
Post High School			-.671	.465	-.892*	.428	-.846*	.426	.055	.056	-.283	.231	-.304	.230
College Graduate			-1.09*	.470	-1.31**	.433	-1.19**	.432	.155**	.056	-.287	.234	-.347	.233
Post College			-.707	.551	-.861+	.508	-.694	.507	.219**	.066	-.196	.274	-.281	.273
Mother's Employment [stay-at-home]														
Fulltime			.284	.330	.340	.304	.308	.302	-.042	.039	.071	.164	.088	.163
Parttime			.027	.379	.180	.349	.168	.348	-.012	.045	.196	.188	.200	.188
Unemployed			.551	.671	.391	.618	.232	.616	-.217**	.080	-.205	.333	-.121	.333
Retired, Welfare, Disabled			.380	.524	.372	.483	.370	.481	-.004	.063	-.010	.260	-.009	.260
Developmental Age [Early Adolescence- 7-8th]														
Middle Adolescence (9-10th Grade)			.020***	.301	-.375	.278	-.398	.276	-.043	.036	-.504***	.149	-.488*	.149
Late Adolescence (11-12th Grade)			1.67***	.360	.997***	.334	.992***	.332	-.026	.043	-.864***	.179	-.854***	.178
Held Back			1.68***	.377	1.41***	.348	1.16***	.351	-.349***	.045	-.341+	.188	-.206	.189

Levels of significance: +p<.10, *p<.05, **p<.01, ***p<.0001

TABLE 5. Continued.

Variable [reference]	Model I		Model II		Model III		Model IV		Model V		Model VI		Model VII	
	b	SD	b	SD	b	SD	b	SD	b	SD	b	SD	b	SD
Race-Ethnicity [non-Hispanic White]														
Non-Hispanic Black			-.241	.393	.365*	.363	.164	.364	-.251***	.047	.774***	.195	.871***	.196
Hispanic			.933*	.371	.790*	.342	.726*	.341	-.090*	.044	-.182	.185	-.147	.184
Non-Hispanic Asian			2.32***	.469	1.92***	.433	1.96***	.431	.041	.056	-.501*	.233	-.517*	.232
Other			.348	.948	.514	.874	.382	.871	-.170	.113	.212	.472	.278	.470
Immigrant Status [native]														
Immigrant			.038	.263	-.051	.242	-.080	.241	-.042	.031	-.113	.131	-.097	.130
Religiosity [not religious]														
Fairly Religious			.018	.316	.064	.291	.056	.290	-.009	.038	.059	.157	.063	.157
Very Religious			.226	.321	.294	.295	.345	.294	.071⁺	.038	.087	.159	.059	.159
Sibling Composition [only child]														
1 Sibling			.539	.372	.676*	.343	.673*	.341	.000	.045	.176	.185	.176	.184
2 Siblings			.664*	.388	.707*	.358	.707*	.356	.001	.046	.054	.193	.054	.192
3 Siblings			.497	.486	.728	.448	.678	.446	-.060	.058	.296	.242	.319	.241
4+ Siblings			-.192	.634	.373	.585	.336	.582	-.033	.076	.722*	.315	.735*	.314
Sexual Experience [virgin]														
Virgin, nonromantic relations			1.18*	.526	1.02*	.485	.840*	.484	-.243***	.063	-.212	.262	-.118	.261
Romantic sex, no nonromantic relations			.356	.463	.241	.428	.137	.427	-.142*	.056	-.146	.231	-.091	.230
Nonromantic sex only			1.44**	.517	1.66***	.476	1.50**	.475	-.208**	.062	-.287	.257	-.368	.256
Romantic sex and nonromantic relations			1.44*	.419	1.58***	.386	1.34*	.388	-.323***	.050	.185	.208	.310	.209
Claims virginity, had romantic sex			.453	.589	.364	.543	.232	.542	-.180*	.071	-.114	.293	-.044	.292
Forced Sexual Experience [never raped]														
Rapist			-.679	1.60	-.054	1.48	.161	1.47	.164	.192	.938	.796	.874	.793
Extracurricular Participation [neither]														
School Club			-.509	.412	-.486	.380	-.326	.379	.214***	.049	.030	.205	-.053	.205
School Athletics			-.856**	.296	-.556*	.273	-.534*	.272	.037	.035	.384*	.147	.370*	.147
Both Club and Athletics			-.828**	.299	-.393	.276	-.196	.278	.277**	.036	.556**	.149	.448**	.150
Relations with Peers														
Quality of Friendships			-1.22***	.154	-.613***	.145	-.623***	.144	.007	.018	.778***	.077	.776***	.076
Body Weight [normal BMI range]														
Overweight			.893*	.348	.429	.321	.370	.320	-.036*	.084	-.594**	.173	-.559**	.172
Underweight			1.07	.699	.653	.644	.635	.642	-.092	.042	-.536	.348	-.522	.346
Intercept	51.82***	1.15	51.73***	1.69	57.26***	1.58	58.65***	1.60	2.02***	.202	7.08***	.838	6.30***	.852
R²	.115		.212		.331		.337		.239		.274		.280	

Levels of significance: ⁺p<.10, *p<.05, **p<.01, ***p<.0001

than non-Hispanic White males (p<.05) although Black adolescents showed no significant difference in comparison to White respondents.

As a whole, sexually experienced adolescents, particularly females, tended to have greater psychological distress than virgins. Having had sex with only a romantic partner (p<.01), having had romantic as well as casual sexual relations (p<.0001), and having had nonromantic sexual relations (p<.05) appeared to put female adolescents at significantly greater risk for depression than virgins. In contrast, males who had nonromantic sex as well as both romantic and casual relations were both significantly more likely to be depressed than males who had never had sex at all (p<.01). Additionally, regressions indicate that female respondents who had been raped suffered emotional anguish (p<.05).

Male athletes, regardless of club membership status, were less likely to be depressed than those respondents who didn't participate in extracurricular activities at all (p<.01) while only girls who were dual club-sports members seemed to benefit, albeit only minimally, from that participation (p<.10). While perceptions of friendship quality were powerfully significant in defending against depression for all adolescents (p<.0001), only boys who were overweight were significantly more likely to suffer from depressive affect than adolescents of normal body mass index (p<.05).

5.3.2. Mediation Regressions (Models III and IV): Introducing self-esteem in female and male sample third models increased variance explained from 21.1% to 33.9% and 21.2% to 33.1%, respectively. As expected, self-esteem was significantly related to depressive affect for both boys and girls (p<.0001), although the coefficient was slightly larger for females (-.876) than males (-.782). The mediation of self-esteem greatly diminished the significance of parent-adolescent attachment. With the exception of mother-son attachment, which lost significance entirely, all coefficients demonstrated that the effects of attachment relations were roughly halved, suggesting partial yet strong mediation. The only significant involvement variable, mother-daughter involvement, was moderately impacted by self-esteem, resulting in a 12% reduction in correlation.

For both samples, the effect of mother's education on depressed mood, as a whole, was weakened while the influence of father's education was slightly strengthened (refer to Tables 4 and 5). The preceding marginal association found between depressive affect and daughters with fulltime working or unemployed mothers as compared to stay-at-home mothers was strengthened in Model III ($p<.05$). Daughters whose mothers were retired, disabled, or on welfare also became significant after self-esteem was added to the regression ($p<.05$).

Self-esteem displayed considerable mediation in regard to adolescent developmental age. In Model III, mid-adolescent males were no longer significantly more depressed than early adolescent males and late adolescent males were less susceptible to psychological difficulties. Likewise, the negative consequences associated with mid-adolescent females disappeared entirely.

Although still significantly more likely to be depressed than White peers, self-esteem attenuated the effect of Asian American status on depressive affect. The presence of self-esteem depleted the strength of the coefficient associated with male (-17%) and female (-16%) Asian teens. Interestingly, the category of African American females developed significant association with depressive symptoms, in which they were estimated to be, on average, one and one-half times more likely to be depressed than White girls (p<.0001). However, the association between Black males and depressed mood remained insignificant. Hispanic adolescent females gained marginal significance associated with increased risk for depression (p<.10) while the coefficient associated with Hispanic males decreased by 15%.

Sibling composition became significant in the male Model III only. Compared to only children, boys with one or two siblings were more likely to be depressed (p<.05), but boys with three or more siblings did not differ significantly from the reference category in risks for depression.

Variable changes associated with sexual experience were inconclusive. For example, within the female sample, self-esteem partially mediated the association between depressive symptomatology and virgins who had had casual sexual relations as well as girls who had been victims of rape. Both associations were weakened in Model III (p<.10). On the other hand, having had romantic sex but no casual sexual relations was strengthened in the latter model (p<.0001). In the male sample, the association between males who had both romantic and casual sexual relations and depressive affect was strengthened slightly (p<.0001).

Overall, extracurricular participation lost considerable associative effect with depressive risk after the inclusion of self-esteem. Participation in both clubs and sports became insignificant in both models while adolescent male athletic status became less significant (p<.05) and declined in correlative power by 35%. Though still extremely salient in protecting both male and female adolescents from depressed mood, perceived friendship quality was nevertheless clearly diluted from Model II to Model III.

Respective male and female friendship quality coefficients corresponded to reductions of 50% and 60%. The preceding significant relationship of being an overweight boy and risk for depression evaporated with the mediation of self-esteem.

Model IV, which introduced academic achievement as an independent variable, resulted in only minimal increases in variance explained for both female (+.009) and male (+.006) models. Grade point average was significantly associated with decreased depressed mood ($p<.0001$), particularly for female adolescents. Within the female sample, academic achievement did not alter the significance of parental relations or self-esteem, but did lower coefficients, albeit only minimally. Female sample Model IV coefficients decreased slightly for maternal attachment (-2.4%), paternal attachment (-8.8%), maternal involvement (-4.7%), and self-esteem (-3.1%).

Although maternal education dummy variables of high school and college educated alike did not change significantly in Model IV, having a mother with a post college education lost considerable correlative strength in Model IV (-18.4%). Correspondingly, the relationships between applicable paternal education variables and daughters' emotional outcomes were also weakened considerably, thus suggesting mediation of adolescent academic achievement. The difference between having a father who graduated from high school and depressive risks, as compared to having a father with no high school diploma, and female adolescent depressed mood became insignificant in Model IV. Also notable, the coefficients associated with post high school and college education dummies resulted in 17.6% and 18.2% reductions correspondingly. However, teenage girls' GPA did not emerge as a mediator in regard to maternal employment status.

In both samples the strength of association between non-Hispanic Black status and depressed mood was weakened due to the mediation of self-esteem. For example, the association between being a Black female, as opposed to a White female, and adolescent depressed mood decreased in significance ($p<.01$) as well as correlative association, which dropped to three-quarters its previous strength. The effect of being a Hispanic teenage girl became insignificant to depressive outcomes once academic achievement was accounted for. In contrast, the Asian status coefficient increased somewhat (+7%).

Two additional variables that appeared to gain relative strength in Model IV included perceptions of being very religious compared to not religious, which became significant ($p<.05$), and being the victim of rape compared to never having been raped ($p<.05$). In general, relevant sexual experience categories were partially mediated by academic achievement (refer to Table 4, Model IV). However, the friendship quality variable remained undisturbed from Model III to Model IV.

Male sample models demonstrated rather trivial mediation in regard to academic achievement and self-esteem (-2.2%). Also within the male sample, grade point average failed to influence the significant relationships between depressed mood and father-son attachment, mid-adolescent standing, Asian status, sibling effects, and quality of friendships. In addition, the regression revealed mixed but minimal mediation pertaining to maternal education, which corresponded with reduced dummy coefficients (2.1% to 6.5%), parental education (5.2% to 9.2% reductions), and Hispanic ethnicity (-8%). As a whole, significant sexual experience categories were significantly, although only partially, mediated by adolescent grade point average (refer to Table 5, Model IV).

5.3.3. *Academic Achievement and Self-Esteem Regressions (Models V, VI, and VII):*

Model V, which replaced depressed mood with academic performance, explained 16.5% of the variance in female depressed mood and 20.2% of the variance in male depressed mood. In general, parental attachment was found to be more powerfully associated with GPA among adolescent females while more involved parents were significant to adolescent male, but not female, GPA. In the former relationships, father-daughter attachment ($p<.01$) was more significant than mother-daughter attachment ($p<.05$) and in the latter relationships, father's involvement ($p<.01$) was more significant than mother's involvement ($p<.10$). Parental educational attainment was positively associated with both boys' and girls' scholastic achievement. As a whole, parental education resulted in slightly stronger association with girls' academic success as compared to boys. Boys with unemployed mothers were at significantly greater risk for poor academic performance than were boys with stay-at-home mothers ($p<.01$). Furthermore, results demonstrated that as maternal and paternal educational attainment increased, the relationship between parental education and GPA became progressively more powerful.

Boys and girls who had been held back in school were significantly more likely to have lower grade point averages than adolescents not held back ($p<.0001$). Only middle adolescent females had significantly lower school grades, on average, than early adolescent females ($p<.01$, $b= -.114$).

Compared to the reference category, non-Hispanic White, non-Hispanic Blacks had significantly lower academic grades regardless of gender ($p<.0001$). Hispanic youth, particularly females ($p<.0001$), had lower school grades than White females while Asian females ($p<.05$) had higher grades than White girls. Perceived religiosity was significantly and positively associated with female GPA, but only marginally positively related to male GPA. As shown in both Model V regressions, sexually active adolescents were found to have significantly lower grades than those adolescents who had remained virgins (refer to Tables 4 & 5, Models V). Males and females who were either club members or dual club-athletic participants had significantly higher grades than peers not involved in extracurricular activities ($p<.01$- $p<.0001$). Being overweight was negatively associated with academic success for both boys ($p<.05$, $b=-.036$) and girls ($p<.01$, $b=-.128$).

In Models VI and VII, I set adolescent self-esteem as the dependent variable. Model VI (no GPA) explained 26.4% of the variance in self-esteem in the female model and 27.4% of the variance in the male model. As displayed in Tables 4 and 5, parental attachment dyads, particularly those of mothers and daughters ($b=.555$), were found to be powerfully associated with higher levels of adolescent self-esteem ($p<.0001$). Although the relationship between father-son attachment and self-esteem ($b=.467$) was more significant than that of father-daughter attachment dyads ($b=.378$), mother-son attachment ($b=.522$) was still slightly more significant to adolescent male self-esteem than father-son attachment. The relationship between cross-sex parental involvement, but not same-sex parental involvement, was highly significant to male self-esteem ($p<.0001$) and somewhat significant to female ($p<.10$) self-esteem.

Maternal educational attainment was found to be significant to males' sense of selves only. On average, a boy whose mother received a high school or GED diploma had significantly higher self-esteem than a same-sex peer whose mother had received no high school education ($p<.05$). Girls with high school educated fathers tended to have slightly poorer self-esteem than those females with fathers who had no high school education. However, the association was only marginally significant (p<.10). Maternal employment status was not found to have any effect on adolescent self-esteem.

Overall, developmental age did contribute to variations in levels of self-esteem among adolescents. Both middle and late adolescent males and females had considerably lower self-esteem than early adolescents. For the sample's females, mid-adolescence was the period found to be most difficult (p<.01, b= -.549) while late adolescence proved to be most emotionally challenging for males (p<.0001, b= -.864). Having been held back in school was significantly more detrimental to female self-esteem (p<.01, b= -.598) than male self-esteem (p<.10, b= .341).

Also shown in Models VI, race was predicative of self-esteem. Compared to the reference category (non-Hispanic White), being African American was positively associated with self-esteem for both girls and boys (p<.0001). In contrast, Asian American adolescents were found to suffer lower levels of self-esteem than peers of other racial-ethnic categories regardless of sex (p<.10- p<.05).

Considering oneself to be very religious, as compared to not religious at all, was associated with higher self-esteem in females (p<.05) while having four or more siblings, as compared to being an only child, was related to higher levels of self-esteem in males (p<.05). Within all sexual activity categories, female virgins who had engaged in nonromantic sexual relations were at three times greater risk for low self-esteem than virgins (p<.05). Any extracurricular involvement that included sports was linked to higher self-esteem for males only (p<.01) while high quality friendships tended to bolster self-esteem for all adolescents (p<.0001). Although an inverse relationship between overweight adolescents and self-esteem was shown for both samples, the effect of overweight status was found to be more detrimental to self-concept stability of females ($p<.0001$, $b= -.935$) than males ($p<.0001$, $b=.594$).

The addition of academic achievement (Model VII) resulted in moderate increases in variance explained by female (+.009) and male (+.006) regressions. Academic achievement was positively associated with adolescent self-esteem in both models ($p<.0001$), but produced a larger coefficient for females (.545) than males (.387). Although none of the dyadic parental attachment relationships were altered significantly by the mediation of adolescent GPA, coefficients attached to father-son involvement (5.8% reduction) and father-daughter involvement (8.3% reduction) were weakened, albeit minimally. In the male sample model VII, the association between the maternal high school and post high school education dummy variables were somewhat weakened, resulting in reductions of 4.6% and 8%, respectively. In contrast, the marginal relationship between high school educated fathers and lower self-esteem among females was strengthened faintly ($p<.05$). Maternal education, however, was not significant to adolescent female self-esteem in either the preceding or the current model.

The association between developmental age and self-esteem was partially mediated by GPA for middle and late adolescent girls, which exhibited corresponding 11% and 5.6% coefficient reductions. However, only trivial mediation emerged in regard to boys. For both models, the relationship between self-esteem and teenagers who had been held back in school was partially mediated by academic achievement, as displayed in lower levels of significance and diminished correlation (refer to Models VII). While coefficients associated with Black status gained strength in both male and female models, none of the other racial categories were affected by the introduction of self-esteem.

The prior significance found within sibling composition and peer relationship variables also did not change from the male sample's Model VI to Model VII. However, male athletic status decreased marginally in associative and correlative significance ($p<.05$, 4% reduction). The relationship between overweight status and self-esteem remained significant at the $p<.01$ level but suffered correlative reduction of 6%. Additional variables within the female sample that demonstrated partial mediation by scholastic performance included being *very religious* (-22.8%) and virgins who had nonromantic sexual relations (-18.9%) (refer to Table 4, Model VII). Perceived friendship quality, however, did not appear to be influenced by adolescent grade point average.

5.3.4. Synopsis of Primary Variable Effects: Split sample models I and II illustrate the importance of parental attachment, particularly that of same-sex parents, to adolescent depressed mood. While all four dyadic attachment relationships were highly significant even after accounting for controls ($p<.0001$), the coefficient related to mother-daughter attachment was over one and one-half times more powerful than that of father-daughter attachment while the representative coefficient for father-son attachment was nearly one and one-half times stronger than that of mother-son attachment (Models II).

The bridge from all dyadic attachment relations to depressive symptoms was attenuated by self-esteem. However, opposite-sex attachment relations were actually more effectively mediated by self-esteem than same-sex attachment relations (Models

III). While the association related to father-daughter attachment was diluted more notably than that of mothers and daughters, mother-son attachment lost significance entirely as a result of self-esteem's introduction.

In model VI regressions, parental attachment was highly significant to adolescent self-esteem outcomes ($p<.0001$). In examining dyadic coefficients within samples, same-sex attachment was found to be one and one-half times more powerful than cross-sex attachment for female self-esteem only. On the other hand, cross-sex attachment was slightly more correlatively significant to sons' self-esteem than same-sex attachment (10% greater).

While adolescent scholastic achievement minimally mediated the relationship between father-daughter attachment and the likelihood for depression, none of the other attachment dyads were affected by GPA (Tables 4-5, Models IV). In concurrence, once academic achievement was set as the outcome variable, father-daughter attachment exhibited stronger significance ($p<.01$) than either mother-daughter ($p<.05$) or mother-son ($p<.10$) attachment (Models V). However, GPA did not emerge as a significant mediator in any of the relationships between parental attachment and self-esteem (Models VII).

Split sample analyses supported full sample analyses in illustrating that parental involvement was considerably less influential to teenagers' emotional and cognitive well-being than parental attachment. In fact, the inclusion of controls alone diminished the significance of involvement variables. Parental involvement did not generate statistical significance in the male sample Model II and only maternal involvement was related to lower depressive affect for girls ($p<.01$).

Self-esteem partially mediated the mother-daughter involvement linkage with depressed mood (11.3% coefficient reduction). GPA did not mediate the aforementioned relationship nor was maternal involvement shown to be significant to adolescent female academic outcomes in Model V. On the other hand, although male respondents' involvement with parents was not markedly significant to adolescent depressive symptomatology, involvement with mothers ($p<.10$) and especially with fathers seemed to inspire sons' academic achievement ($p<.01$). In general, cross-sex parent-adolescent involvement was more powerfully associated with adolescent self-esteem than same-sex involvement. Of all dyadic involvement relationships, only those of mother-son ($p<.01$) and father-daughter ($p<.10$) were significantly linked to adolescent self-esteem (Models VI). The above referenced involvement relations showed negligible GPA mediation in Model VII.

5.4. Interaction Regression Analyses

In order to corroborate baseline models, I implemented supplemental regressions to interact parent-adolescent relationship quality domains with adolescent gender[2]. I examined interactive effects on depressed mood as well as self-esteem (models available upon request). Models were significant at the .0001 levels and, overall, illustrated some notable gender differentials.

---

[2] $Y=b_0 + b_1\text{Parent-Adolescent Attachment/Involvement} + b_2 \text{Adolescent Gender} + b_3\text{Parent-Adolescent Attachment/InvolvementXGender}$

5.4.1. Full Sample Parent-Child Relations and Adolescent Gender Interactions:

The first two models focused on the association between dyadic parent-adolescent relationship domains and depressed mood. Of these four models, only those pertaining to relationships with mothers demonstrated significant interaction effects. Interactive terms focusing on maternal attachment by adolescent sex (p=.024) as well as mother's involvement by sex (p=.045) highlighted mother-daughter relations over mother-son relations. Restricting the aforementioned attachment analysis by gender produced coefficients of -.84 for females and -.55 for males, which displayed the augmented import of maternal attachment to daughters' depressed mood. The involvement model's corresponding coefficients demonstrated that the association between mother's involvement and depressed mood was three times more powerful for female adolescents (b= -.691) than for male adolescents (b= -.227). On the other hand, children's attachment relations with fathers failed to interact significantly with adolescent gender. However, considering that attachment relationships with fathers were significant in baseline models, the lack of results only suggest that neither daughters nor sons were significantly more dependent on paternal attachment than the other sex.

Next, I conducted interaction regression analyses that scrutinized adolescent self-esteem instead of depressed mood. Results were not as robust as previous models, but exposed significant interactive effects nonetheless. Surprisingly, attachment to mothers was not found to vary significantly once the analysis was restricted by gender. Instead, self-esteem interactive models revealed that the association between paternal attachment and self-esteem varied significantly, even if only marginally, by gender (p=.079). Upon restrictions, perceived attachment with fathers was positively correlated with both male and female adolescent self-esteem. However, resultant coefficients showed that paternal involvement was more significant to boys' self-esteem ($b=.461$) than girls' self-esteem ($b=.380$). When involvement relations were interacted on adolescent sex, maternal involvement, but not paternal involvement, displayed a significant interactive term ($p=.0616$). In this case, cross-sex mother-son involvement ($b=.259$) was found to be more strongly linked to adolescent self-esteem than same-sex mother-daughter involvement ($b=.054$).

5.4.2. Full Sample Parent-Child Relations and Adolescent Age Interactions:

In order to explore important age-related implications, I incorporated necessary interactive terms on the full sample of adolescents (Parent-Adolescent Relationship Domains X Age)[3]. Although all eight regression models were significant at the $p<.0001$ levels, only one exhibited significant interactive effects. The association between attachment to fathers and adolescent self-esteem was found to be most significantly correlated during early adolescence. When the interaction analysis was restricted by developmental age, father-adolescent attachment was found to interact most persuasively with early adolescent self-esteem ($b=.593$) as compared to middle ($b=.4170$) and late adolescents ($b=.4064$) (model available upon request).

---

[3] $Y = b_0 + b_1$Parent-Adolescent Attachment/Involvement + b_2 Mid-Adolescents (9/10th graders) + b_3 Late Adolescents (11/12th graders) + b_4 Held Back + b_5Parent-Adolescent Attachment/InvolvementX9/10th + b_6Parent-Adolescent Attachment/InvolvementX11/12th + b_7Parent-Adolescent Attachment/InvolvementXHeldBack

5.4.3. Split Sample Parent-Child Relations and Adolescent Age Interactions:

Given the clear discrepancies that emerged in cross-sectional models in regard to adolescent gender, I determined that interacting parental relations on adolescent age through only full sample models was insufficient. To fortify analyses, I extended the investigation to account for distinct male and female developmental age implications. In doing so, separate male and female interaction models were analyzed and more detailed findings materialized.[4] All sixteen regressions were highly significant (p<.0001). In analyses of adolescent girls' depressive symptoms, only maternal involvement interacted with developmental age significantly (p=.0586). Despite its nominal level of statistical significance, after restricting the analysis middle adolescent females were found to be considerably more impacted by perceptions of maternal involvement (-1.05) than were early adolescent peers (-.233) (models available upon request). The depressed mood interaction models based on the male sample failed to produce notable interaction effects.

In self-esteem models, the effect of adolescent age was found to be particularly significant in regard to parental attachment and self-esteem. Results demonstrated that both maternal and paternal attachment were significantly more powerfully associated with daughters of early adolescent age than late adolescent age. When mother-daughter attachment was interacted on developmental age, the late adolescent interactive term exhibited a p-value of .016. Once restricted, ensuing coefficients suggested that the youngest females were significantly more dependent on maternal attachment ($b=.630$) than the oldest cohort of females ($b=.363$). Similar, albeit somewhat weaker results emerged pertaining to paternal attachment. When I interacted father-daughter attachment

---

[4] $Y = b_0 + b_1$Parent-Adolescent Attachment/Involvement $+ b_2$ Mid-Adolescents (9/10th graders) $+ b_3$ Late Adolescents (11/12th graders) $+ b_4$ Held Back $+ b_5$Parent-Adolescent Attachment/InvolvementX9/10th $+ b_6$Parent-Adolescent Attachment/InvolvementX11/12th $+ b_7$Parent-Adolescent Attachment/InvolvementXHeldBack

on self-esteem, the late adolescent interactive term was marginally significant (p=.067) and exhibited a post-restriction coefficient of .302. In contrast, the resulting early adolescent reference variable displayed a coefficient of .468. In sum, results established the enhanced significance of youngest, 7th to 8th grade female attachment relationships with both parents as compared to their oldest, 11th to 12th grade counterparts.

Of the four interaction regressions based on the male sample, only the relationship between father-son attachment and adolescent self-esteem appeared to be age dependent. Interactive terms associated with mid-adolescents (p=.067) as well as late adolescents (p=.077) achieved marginal significance. Similar to female youth, same-sex attachment was most pronounced to adolescent self-esteem at the beginning of the developmental period. After restrictions, boys of the early adolescent developmental stage exhibited greater association (b=.593) than same-sex peers in middle adolescence (b=.417) and late adolescence (b=.406) (models available upon request).

5.5. Strength of Paired Correlation Z-Tests

Paired correlation analyses were employed to examine the implications of adolescent developmental age on parent-teen relationships and adolescent psychosocial health both within and between samples. Table 6 shows computed z-tests for parental attachment and involvement on adolescent male and female depressed mood. Table 7 demonstrates results of parallel paired correlation analyses relating to adolescent self-esteem. After transforming respective bivariate correlations (r) into z-values, I compared the strength of correlations within each sample as well as between samples using the following z-test formulas:

Within Sample:	Between Samples:
$$\dfrac{Z_1 - Z_2}{\sqrt{1/N-3 + 1/N-3}}$$	$$\dfrac{Z_F - Z_M}{\sqrt{1/N_F-3 + 1/N_M-3}}$$

5.5.1. Depressed Mood: In general, Table 6 z-values illustrate that, for females, although attachment to both parents was reported to be highly significantly to psychological health, paternal attachment was more significant than maternal attachment during early adolescence. However, maternal attachment was more significant than paternal attachment for older, middle adolescent girls. Within the male sample, paternal attachment was most significant to boys' depressive state during early adolescence.

Closer examination of within-sample analyses revealed that maternal and paternal attachment relations were equally salient to daughters' mood disturbance. However, results of male within-sample tests emphasized same-sex relationship attachment. Paternal attachment was more significant than cross-sex attachment for the entire male sample ($p<.0001$) and marginally significant for those boys who were early adolescents ($p<.10$), late adolescents ($p<.10$), and who had been held back a grade in school ($p<.10$).

Total between-sample models demonstrated that relationships with mothers, in terms of attachment ($p<.0001$) as well as involvement ($p<.05$), were most significantly associated with girls' depressive symptomatology. Likewise, paired correlation analyses of middle adolescents illustrated that maternal attachment ($p<.05$) and involvement ($p<.01$) were more significant to depressive risks among daughters than sons. Furthermore, father-daughter involvement during the same period was found to be more influential to adolescent depressive outcomes than father-son involvement ($p<.05$).

Table 6. Strength of paired correlation Z-tests of parent-adolescent relationship and depressed mood by adolescent sex and developmental age.

		Female Adolescents								Male Adolescents						
		Attachment			Involvement					Attachment			Involvement			
Sample	N	Mother Z	Father Z	Within N Critical Z	Mother Z	Father Z	Within N Critical Z		N	Mother Z	Father Z	Within N Critical Z	Mother Z	Father Z	Within N Critical Z
Total	2,625	-.334***	-.334***	.000	-.201***	-.182***	.688		2,440	-.243***	-.318***	-2.62**	-.143***	-.161***	-.629
Early Adolescents (7th-8th Graders)	758	-.310***	-.334***	-.471	-.135**	-.164***	-.569		663	-.268***	-.343***	-1.36⁺	-.106**	-.151***	-.818
Middle Adolescents (9th-10th Graders)	996	-.341***	-.325***	.356	-.217***	-.168***	1.09		847	-.249***	-.301***	-1.08	-.078*	-.084*	.125
Late Adolescents (11th-12th Graders)	585	-.275***	-.303***	-.478	-.178***	-.157**	.358		496	-.224***	-.316***	-1.44⁺	-.121**	-.125**	-.063
Held Back Adolescents (Stayed Back in School)	286	-.343***	-.279***	.080	-.164**	-.110	.643		434	-.145**	-.234***	-1.31⁺	-.123*	-.129*	.088

Levels of bivariate correlational (r) significance: p≤.05*, p≤.01**, p≤.0001***

Significant Between Sample Findings:

Total Sample	Crit Z
Maternal Attachment	-3.25**
Maternal Involvement	-2.07*

Mid-Adolescents	
Maternal Attachment	-1.97*
Maternal Involvement	-2.97**
Paternal Involvement	-1.79*

Held Back Adolescents	
Maternal Attachment	-2.59**

Table 7. Strength of paired correlation Z-tests of parent-adolescent relationship and self-esteem by adolescent sex and developmental age.

		Female Adolescents								Male Adolescents						
		Attachment			Involvement				Attachment			Involvement			
Sample	N	Mother Z	Father Z	Within N Critical Z	Z	Z	Within N Critical Z	N	Mother Z	Father Z	Within N Critical Z	Mother Z	Father Z	Within N Critical Z
Total	2,625	.421***	.405***	.580	.149***	.171***	-.797	2,440	.382***	.417***	-1.22	.174***	.161***	.455
Early Adolescents (7th-8th Graders)	758	.431***	.436***	-.098	.131**	.184***	-1.04	663	.421***	.492***	-1.31+	.133**	.178***	-.833
Middle Adolescents (9th-10th Graders)	996	.419***	.402***	.379	.139***	.153***	-.312	847	.382***	.388***	-.125	.121**	.078*	.896
Late Adolescents (11th-12th Graders)	585	.305***	.321***	-.273	.104*	.131**	-.461	496	.359***	.356***	.047	.145**	.182**	.581
Held Back Adolescents (Stayed Back in School)	286	.539***	.409***	1.55**	.145*	.080	-.774	434	.281***	.377***	-1.41+	.178**	.168**	.147

Levels of bivariate correlational (r) significance: p<.05*, p<.01**, p<.0001***

Significant Between Sample Findings:

	Crit Z
Total Sample	
Maternal Attachment	1.39+
Mid-Adolescents	
Paternal Involvement	1.60+
Held Back Adolescents	
Maternal Attachment	3.37***

Comparing male and female samples of adolescents who had been held back in school demonstrated that maternal attachment was more significant to the psyches of females than males in this particular segment of adolescents (p<.01).

As a whole, within and between sample analyses of parent-adolescent relations and depressed mood draw attention to same-sex parent-child attachment relationships. Moreover, analyses suggest that, in general, parental relationships are more salient to the depressive outcomes of girls than boys.

5.5.2. *Self-Esteem*: Paired correlation analyses of self-esteem are exhibited in Table 7. Basic review of reported z-values demonstrates the importance of both mother's and father's attachment to early adolescents in particular. Overall, the results of the analysis illustrate that attachment to parents becomes increasingly less important through middle and late adolescence. Within samples, both males (p<.10) and females (p<.01) who had been held back were found to depend significantly more on same-sex parental attachment than opposite-sex attachment. Consistent with Table 6 z-tests, girls' self-esteem was not found to be significantly more contingent on relations with either parent as compared to the other. Within the male sample, computations showed only early adolescent male self-esteem to be associated more strongly with paternal attachment than maternal attachment (p<.10).

Between sample z-tests illustrated girls' increased dependence on relationships with parents for self-esteem enhancement. In examining strength of correlations between male and female adolescent self-esteem and relationships with mothers, the total samples and held back samples were both significant at the p<.10 and p<.0001 levels, respectively. Both upheld that mother attachment was more significant to self-esteem outcomes of daughters than sons. None of the other age-graded samples revealed significant gender differences in maternal relationship domains. The only noteworthy finding to emerge in between-sample analyses regarding father-adolescent dyads pertained to paternal involvement. For mid-adolescents, z-values correlating paternal relationship involvement and adolescent self-esteem were significantly more powerful for adolescent females than males (p=.055). With the exception of this last finding that stressed father-daughter dyads, all other results presented same-sex parent-adolescent relationships to be more significant to adolescent self-esteem than cross-sex relations.

5.6. Longitudinal Regression Analyses

Phase II longitudinal regressions investigated the stability and variability in primary variables over the course of one year (Table 8). Longitudinal methods advanced cross-sectional findings of association in providing analysis of causal processes that led to emotional disturbance in the present sample of respondents over time. In total, I ran twelve longitudinal models, all of which were significant at p<.0001 levels. First, for each adolescent sample, all Wave 1 variables (including depressed mood) were regressed on adolescent depressed mood at time 2 (Model I). As reported in Table 8, these models explained 38% of the variance in time 2 adolescent female depressed mood and 35.9% of the variance in the corresponding male model.

5.6.1. Depressed Mood: As expected, models revealed that depressed mood was stable over the course of the year for youth of both sexes (p<.0001). Coefficients suggest that depressed mood at time 1 worsened depressed symptomatology over time. In addition, both self-esteem and academic achievement predicted depressed mood at time 2 ($p<.01$). Self-esteem was shown to be similarly significant to male and female depressed mood, exhibiting correlations of -.135 and -.137, respectively (Models I). Grade point average, on the other hand, was revealed to be more salient to females than males. Of all dyadic parent-adolescent relationship domains, only father-daughter attachment was found to influence later depressed mood ($p<.0001$). Higher paternal attachment seemed to insulate girls from emotional disturbance ($b=-.376$).

Of parental demographic variables associated with females, post college educated fathers compared to fathers with no high school education ($b=-1.05$) and fully employed mothers compared to stay-at-home mothers ($b=-.613$) contributed minimally to lower depressive affect. Likewise, boys' resultant depressive affect was only marginally benefited by having a father with some form of post high school education as compared to no high school education ($b=-.847$). In sum, the only dyadic relationship to produce significance over time was that of father-daughter attachment, which was found to protect adolescent females from depressive risks.

TABLE 8. Ordinary least squares longitudinal analyses regressing Time 1 variables on Time 2 adolescent depressed mood and self-esteem.

| | Female Sample (N=2,625) | | | | Male Sample (N=2,440) | | | |
| | Model I Depressed Mood (T2) | | Model II Self-Esteem (T2) | | Model I Depressed Mood (T2) | | Model II Self-Esteem (T2) | |
Time 1 Variables [reference]	b	SD	b	SD	b	SD	b	SD
Primary								
Mother-Adolescent Attachment	.140	.086	.105**	.040	-.101	.106	.158**	.055
Father-Adolescent Attachment	-.376***	.070	.115**	.032	-.109	.080	.091*	.041
Maternal Involvement	.049	.180	-.009	.084	.060	.163	.038	.085
Paternal Involvement	-.085	.156	.084	.073	-.182	.137	-.013	.071
Depressed Mood	.493***	.019	-.014	.009	.509***	.021	-.061***	.011
Self-Esteem	-.117**	.041	.467***	.019	-.135**	.042	.424***	.022
Academic Achievement	-.658**	.186	.175*	.086	-.430**	.163	.165+	.084
Controls								
Parental Education [no high school]								
Mother: High School	.698	.424	-.308	.197	.058	.416	-.025	.216
Post High School	.478	.469	-.188	.218	-.291	.467	.254	.243
College Graduate	.726	.492	-.551*	.229	-.213	.474	.135	.247
Post College	.530	.609	-.486*	.283	.209	.588	-.004	.306
Father: High School	-.270	.408	.160	.190	-.378	.397	.243	.207
Post High School	-.580	.452	.112	.210	-.847+	.440	.155	.229
College Graduate	-.726	.463	.376*	.215	-.537	.447	-.041	.232
Post College	-1.05+	.539	.311	.251	-.652	.523	-.005	.272
Mother's Employment [stay-at-home]								
Fulltime	-.613+	.327	.121	.152	-.056	.312	.144	.162
Parttime	-.585	.391	-.117	.182	-.305	.359	.274	.186
Unemployed	-.471	.680	.427	.316	.700	.360	-.278	.329
Retired, Welfare, Disabled	-.070	.519	-.102	.241	-.102	.496	.606*	.257
Developmental Age [Early Adolescence]								
Middle Adolescence (9-10th Grade)	.006	.230	-.112	.137	.672*	.285	-.248+	.148
Late Adolescence (11-12th Grade)	-.020	.352	-.049	.164	.252	.344	-.234	.178
Held Back	-.207	.440	.028	.205	.589	.363	-.367+	.188
Race-Ethnicity [non-Hispanic White]								
Non-Hispanic Black	.017	.370	.758***	.172	-.034	.376	.112	.194
Hispanic	.477	.376	-.483**	.175	.490	.352	.038	.183
Non-Hispanic Asian	2.04**	.540	-.283	.250	.671	.447	-.381+	.232
Other	1.10	1.22	-.907	.566	.861	.90	.016	.465
Immigrant [native]	.272	.263	-.122	.122	.140	.249	.020	.129
Fairly Religious	-.494	.349	-.204	.162	-.291	.299	.316*	.155
Very Religious	-.066	.345	-.003	.160	-.637*	.304	.482**	.157
Sibling Composition [only child]								
1 Sibling	.181	.405	-.278	.188	.145	.353	.091	.183
2 Siblings	-.058	.425	-.151	.197	.415	.368	-.013	.190
3 Siblings	.128	.501	-.095	.233	.405	.461	-.226	.238
4+ Siblings	.196	.638	.246	.297	.090	.601	.324	.311
Sexual Experience [virgin]								
Virgin, nonromantic relations	.625	.871	.132	.405	-.151	.500	.287	.259
Romantic sex, no nonromantic relations	-.163	.426	.280	.198	.354	.440	.425+	.228
Nonromantic sex only	1.68*	.737	.250	.343	.257	.492	.725**	.254
Romantic sex and nonromantic relations	-.563	.457	.614**	.212	.679+	.402	.326	.208
Claims virginity, had romantic sex	.021	.707	.184	.328	.116	.559	.172	.289
Victim (female), Rapist (male)[never raped]	.300	.661	.337	.307	4.44**	1.52	-.582	.785

Levels of significance: +p<.10, *p<.05, **p<.01, ***p<.0001

TABLE 8. Continued

Time 1 Variables [reference]	Female Sample (N=2,625)				Male Sample (N=2,440)			
	Model I Depressed Mood (T2)		Model II Self-Esteem (T2)		Model I Depressed Mood (T2)		Model II Self-Esteem (T2)	
	b	SD	b	SD	b	SD	b	SD
Extracurricular Participation [neither]								
School Club	-.693*	.317	.070	.147	-.572	.392	.346⁻	.203
School Athletics	.980*	.455	-.261	.212	.127	.281	.371*	.146
Both Club and Athletics	-.457	.286	.198	.133	.015	.287	.324*	.149
Relations with Peers								
Quality of Friendships	-.396*	.176	.318***	.082	-.099	.150	.080	.077
Body Weight [normal BMI range]								
Overweight	-.139	.457	-.183	.211	.163	.330	-.502**	.171
Underweight	-.813	.734	.410	.341	-.297	.662	.016	.343
Intercept	25.06***	2.01	9.01***	.932	22.43***	2.06	11.56***	1.07
R2	.380		.375		.359		.332	

Levels of significance: ⁻p<.10, *p<.05, **p<.01, ***p<.0001

The rest of the regressions revealed sporadic significance. For example, being a mid-adolescent male at time 1 ($p<.05$) or admitting to having committed rape ($p<.01$) were both related to increased depressive symptomatology at time 2. In fact, rapists were nearly four times as likely as non-rapists to suffer later depressed mood. Race did not predict depressed mood at time 2 for males, but Asian females were over twice as likely as White females to experience negative psychological states at time 2 ($p<.01$).

Regressions demonstrated that females who reported having nonromantic sex, but no romantic sex at time 1 were at significantly greater risk for developing later depressed mood than were virgin females ($p<.05$). Males who claimed to have had both romantic and casual sex at time 1 were slightly more likely to experience depressed mood one year later than males who were sexually inexperienced ($p<.10$). Compared to girls who did not participate in extracurricular activities at all, club membership seemed to benefit psychological outcomes ($p<.05$, $b=-.693$) while athletic status adversely affected girls' later emotional states ($p<.05$, $b=.980$). Finally, although higher reported friendship quality seemed to protect girls from depressive affect ($p<.05$), friendships were not found to predict adolescent male psychological outcomes.

5.6.2. Self-Esteem: Model II regressed time 1 variables on time 2 adolescent self-esteem (see Table 8, Models II). The computed R-square was larger for the female sample (.375) than the male sample (.332). Time 1 self-esteem ($p<.0001$) and time 1 GPA ($p<.05$ for females, $p<.10$ for males) were found to be promote subsequent self-esteem in both samples. However, findings suggest that time 1 self-esteem and time 1 scholastic performance were more salient to female than male self-concepts. However, depressed mood was found to contribute to worsening self-esteem for males (p<.0001), but not females. Parental attachment relationships, but not parental involvement, were found to enhance children's later self-esteem. All attachment relations exhibited significant beta coefficients (p<.01), except for father-son attachment, which was significant at the p<.05 level. Overall, parental attachment relationship quality positively impacted adolescent self-concept development while parental involvement did not demonstrate causal association. While the influence of mother and father attachment relations were found to equitably influence female self-esteem over time, longitudinal regressions illustrated that maternal attachment boosted sons' self-esteem slightly more than did father-son attachment.

Parental education was not found to predict changes in sons' self-esteem, but the highest levels of maternal educational attainment, college and post college, were shown to lower daughters' sense of selves over time (p<.05 and p<.10, respectively). Conversely, having fathers with college diplomas heightened daughters' self-esteem, but only marginally (p<.10).

Compared to respective reference variables, adolescent male self-esteem was impaired by mid-adolescence (p<.10), being held back in school (p<.10), Asian status (p<.10), and being overweight (p<.01). Conversely, regressions indicated that male self-esteem was enhanced by beliefs of being fairly religious (p<.05) or very religious (p<.01), engaging in only romantic (p<.10) or only nonromantic (p<.05) sexual activity, and school club (p<.10), athletic (p<.05), or dual participation (p<.05). Analysis of coefficients indicates that perceptions of friendships significantly and positively impacted female self-esteem over time (p<.001), but did not predict changes in male adolescent self-esteem. Contrary to cross-sectional models, the present analysis found that after controlling for time 1 self-esteem, girls who had romantic and nonromantic sexual relations at time 1 had heightened self-esteem one year later ($p<.01$). Race variables revealed discrepancies for females. Although being a Black female was associated with increased self-esteem over time ($p<.0001$), being Hispanic had negative ramifications for adolescent female teens' future emotional states ($p<.01$).

5.6.3. *Parent-Adolescent Relationship Domains*: The eight longitudinal regression models that assessed whether adolescent perceptions of dyadic parental attachment and involvement would remain stable or would fluctuate over the course of a year exhibited clear and consistent results. All models were highly significant ($p<.0001$) and demonstrated that, during adolescence, boys' and girls' relations with mothers and fathers remained relatively stable.

In regard to the adolescent female sample, time 1 maternal attachment, paternal attachment, maternal involvement, and paternal involvement were all highly correlated with time 2 complements ($p<.0001$), and exhibited positive coefficient estimates of .524, .607, .236, and .378, respectively. Similarly, time 1 and time 2 parent-son relationship domains were powerfully associated ($p<.0001$), revealing positive beta coefficients for perceived attachment with both mothers ($b=.524$) and fathers ($b=.610$) as well as perceived maternal ($b=.209$) and paternal ($b=.346$) involvement. Associations were similar for both samples (models available upon request).

CHAPTER SIX
DISCUSSION

6.1. Cross-Sectional Analyses

Although analyses supported that all parent-adolescent relationships were fundamental to adolescent depressed mood, self-esteem, and academic achievement, specific dyadic pairings proved to have distinct and powerful relationships with boys' and girls' emotional and cognitive outcomes. Most hypotheses were generally supported by statistical findings.

6.1.1. Adolescent Depressed Mood

As expected, analyses maintained that adolescent girls were at greater risk for depression than adolescent boys. For the most part, full sample regressions upheld the first hypothesis:

H1. Although each parent-adolescent relationship domain should be inversely associated with adolescent depressed mood, parent-adolescent attachment should be a stronger buffer against depressed mood than parental involvement.

All parent-teen relationship domains were inversely associated with depressed mood in Model I, although father-adolescent involvement lost its significance once controls were introduced. Nevertheless, parent-child attachment was clearly more powerfully associated with depressed mood than parental involvement in all depression models.

Findings support developmental theories of attachment that emphasize the importance of close and supportive parent-adolescent relationships to children's psychosocial development (Bowlby 1958, 1982; Noom et al. 1999; Sartor & Youniss 2002). The emotional component of parent-adolescent attachment is shown to be more intimately tied to children's emotional and expressive outcomes than the behavioral component of parental involvement. Parental attachment seems to provide essential psychological security for children during adolescence, a critical developmental period of newfound independence and interpersonal exploration. In effect, healthy attachment relations foster competent internal working models and self-understanding which promote social functioning, independence, and resiliency. Clearly, such mental frameworks are essential to psychological well-being.

In accordance with the second hypothesis, same-sex parents were generally found to be more significant to both male and female adolescent depressive risks than were cross-sex parents:

H2. Same-sex parent-adolescent relationship domains are expected to be stronger predictors of adolescent depressed mood than cross-sex parent-adolescent relationship domains.

Current findings corroborate contemporary psychoanalytic theory that sets mother-daughter and father-son dyads as essential to the healthy development of gender identity (Chodorow 1978). Such identification theories contend that, from infancy, children internalize the behaviors and values of their same-sex parent, who becomes the primary role model by which the child perceives himself or herself as a person. The significance of same-sex dyads found in this analysis supports that, despite increased detachment, same-sex parents are still essential points of reference for adolescents.

Adolescence marks a period in which teenagers are faced with cultural pressure to comply with appropriate gender identities. Therefore, it is not surprising that same-sex parents become more significant to adolescent depressed mood than cross-sex parents during this life stage. This book demonstrates that amid such gender intensification, same-sex parent-child relationships become most central to adolescents.

The present study also substantiated Hypothesis 3:

H3. *Adolescent female depressed mood should be more dependent on relationships with both cross-sex and same-sex parents than adolescent male depressed mood.*

Based on split sample cross-sectional, interactive, and between-sample paired correlation analyses, I contend that attachment and involvement with parents, particularly same-sex parents, are most salient to relationship-oriented daughters. Results also indicate that cross-sex parents were more predicative of female than male depressive risks. In fact, the sole dyadic parent-teen relationship to surface as significant in longitudinal analyses was that of father-daughter attachment.

Despite the comparatively weaker connection between parental involvement and depressive outcomes, mother-daughter involvement did consistently generate significant association in cross-sectional regression and paired correlation analyses. More specifically, involvement with mothers seemed to become most salient to female affective state during middle adolescence. As shown in paired correlation tests, even involvement with fathers was more significant to mid-adolescent females than it was to male counterparts during that particular developmental period. However, dyadic involvement variables failed to demonstrate causal influences on adolescent depressed mood in longitudinal models. By and large, analyses established daughters' greater dependency on both relationship domains of same-sex and opposite-sex parents as compared to sons.

Results are consistent with models of primary feminine identification and gender socialization that account for female orientations to interpersonal connections and intimacy (Chodorow 1974, 1978; Gilligan 1982). Throughout childhood girls are socialized to value relationships and connectedness while boys are taught to be more individualistic and independent (Beutel & Marini 1995; Fischer et al. 1989). Clearly, relationships with significant others are more psychologically central to female self-concepts than male sense of selves. By adolescence, children embody differential self-definitions, in which females espouse interdependent definitions and males tend to define themselves in terms of independence (Kohlberg 1966; Kondo 1990). Considering girls' relationship-oriented dispositions, results that highlight the greater import of both same-sex and cross-sex relationships to female teens as compared to male teens are not surprising.

6.1.2. Adolescent Self-Esteem

The first hypothesis relating to mediation analyses posited the following:

H4. Most of the association between parent-adolescent relationship domains and adolescent depressed mood should be explained by the mediation of adolescent self-esteem.

Self-esteem proved to be a powerful partial mediator of the relationship between parent-child relations and teenagers' depressed mood. In concurrence with predictions, self-esteem mediated the bridge between parental attachment and depressed mood quite substantially. However, in regard to parental involvement, self-esteem did not mediate "most" of the association. Therefore, findings can only moderately support Hypothesis 4.

In sum, the evidence presented in this book advocates Beck's cognitive model of depression (1967), which sets self-esteem as antecedent to depressed mood. The strong attenuating effects of adolescent self-esteem demonstrate that self-esteem is a fundamental source of depressed mood. More specifically, current findings are consistent with studies that have investigated the mediating role that self-esteem plays in the relationship between parent-child interaction and psychological health (Brown & Harris 1978; Wilkinson 2004).

The next hypothesis stated the following:

H5. Self-esteem should be a stronger mediator in the relationship between dyadic parent-adolescent attachment and depressed mood than the relationship between parental involvement and depressed mood.

While self-esteem was strongly associated with all parent-child relationship domains, it was especially salient to attachment relations. Although Hypothesis 5 could not be tested thoroughly due to lack of association between paternal involvement and depressed mood, it was supported by the significant maternal involvement variables. In full sample and female sample models, self-esteem attenuated the effect of both attachment relations to a much greater degree than maternal involvement.

The theoretical explanation pertaining to the first hypothesis is germane to the fifth hypothesis. Again, parental attachment is illustrated to be exceedingly salient to the psychosocial dimensions of teens' well-being. During a time when a child is confronting challenges of identity negotiation, healthy attachment to parents is shown to reinforce a teenager's sense of worth and self-esteem. Findings support that as adolescents detach from parents in search for autonomy and self-concept definition, having close and positive connections with primary significant others becomes increasingly vital to adolescent self-esteem. All in all, the affective-oriented attachment variables are found to be more salient to adolescent self-concept than the instrumental-oriented involvement variables.

Overall, Hypothesis 6 was not fully confirmed:

H6. Same-sex parent-adolescent relationship attachment and involvement should be stronger predictors of adolescent self-esteem than cross-sex parent-adolescent relationship domains.

Compared to prior regressions that demonstrated the enhanced salience of same-sex parent-child relations over cross-sex dyads for both female and male depressive risks, regressions that incorporated self-esteem were less consistent. First, mediation regressions illustrated that although self-esteem similarly mediated the relationship between each parent-daughter attachment relationship and adolescent depressed mood, self-esteem attenuated more of the effect of mother-son attachment than father-son attachment. Furthermore, regressions in which self-esteem represented the outcome variable revealed mother-daughter attachment to be the only same-sex dyadic relationship conclusively more influential than its cross-sex counterpart. In contrast to predictions, paternal involvement was marginally associated with female self-esteem while maternal involvement was insignificant.

Overall, the relationship between parent-son attachment and adolescent boys' self-esteem produced inconsistent results. Although mother-son and father-son attachment relations were comparable in male sample cross-sectional regressions, the former attachment relationship produced a slightly stronger coefficient (+11.2%). Maternal attachment was also slightly more significant than paternal attachment in longitudinal analyses. Further, maternal involvement was significant to boys' self-esteem while paternal involvement was not. However, paired correlation tests demonstrated that adolescent male attachment to fathers was significantly more influential than attachment to mothers during early adolescence and for those boys held back in school. Paired correlation analyses thus suggest that same-sex identification becomes most relevant to sons' self-esteem during periods in which self-concepts tend to be most challenged.

Contrary to literature that fails to appreciate the role of cross-sex parent-child relationships to adolescent self-concept development, the present analyses demonstrated the import of cross-sex relations to male and female adolescent self-concept trajectories. On one hand, findings conflict with modern psychoanalytic theories of parental identification by emphasizing maternal-oriented self-concept development for not only daughters, but sons as well. On the other hand, the fact that attachment to fathers was most significant to sons' self-esteem during early adolescence evokes the possibility that same-sex parental identification is in fact most significant to sons, but only when boys are most insecure about their identities.

Hypothesis 7 was supported:

H7. Same-sex and cross-sex parent-adolescent relations should be more strongly associated with girls' self-esteem than boys' self-esteem.

Cross-sectional models substantiated that self-esteem was a critical source of females' significantly higher rates of depression as compared to males. Although all dyadic attachment relations were highly significant to self-concepts of girls as well as boys, full sample paired correlation analyses illustrated that same-sex and cross-sex relations were most influential to girls' depressive symptomatology (Table 7). Also in concurrence with the seventh hypothesis, girls' relations with mothers were more powerful to self-esteem than boys' relations with fathers. Moreover, despite the significance of mother-son relationships, female adolescents' connections with fathers were found to be more significant to adolescent self-esteem than male adolescents' connections to mothers. In fact, as exhibited in paired correlation z-test analyses, paternal involvement was more significant to mid-adolescent female self-esteem than mid-adolescent male self-esteem.

This book's results challenge literature that conveys father-daughter relationships to be the least emotionally involved of all parent-child dyads (Dornbusch, 1989; Steinberg, 1987). Regression models and between-sample paired correlation z-tests clearly illustrate early adolescent girls' connections with their fathers. In sum, analyses suggest that adolescent girls are more dependent on emotional attachment and appraisals reflected from not only same-sex parents, but also cross-sex parents than are adolescent boys.

Results were anticipated given that female self-concepts tend to be linked to emotional support, intimate relationships, and self-definition while male self-concepts are most dependent on achievement, status, and self-attribution (Eder & Hallihan 1978; Lord & Eccles 1994; Verkuyten 2003). Females are socialized to have interdependent self-construals in which the self is defined through connectedness with others (Cross & Madson 1997). When adolescents negotiate their identities in relation to others, such gender orientations become extremely salient. In recognizing girls' preoccupation with maintaining close and intimate connections with others, it is no surprise that both same-sex and cross-sex parental relations were most integral to teenage girls' psychosocial health as compared to boys.

The final hypothesis relating to self-esteem was confirmed:

H8. Of all dyadic parent-adolescent relations, those between mothers and daughters should exhibit the strongest association with self-esteem outcomes.

In corroboration with the majority of child development literature, of all dyadic pairings those between mothers and daughters were found to be most consistently salient to adolescent self-esteem. Rooted in primary feminine identification, contemporary psychoanalysis emphasizes girls' deep connections with their mothers. Current findings that clearly place mother-daughter relationships as most vital to adolescent self-esteem are consistent with the vast majority of child development literature.

6.1.3. Adolescent Academic Achievement

On average, girls performed better scholastically than boys. Overall, academic achievement demonstrated minimal mediation at best. Therefore, while analyses agree with Hypothesis 9, it cannot be decisively confirmed:

H9. Academic achievement should partially mediate the association between parent-adolescent relationship domains and adolescent self-esteem.

In sum, scholastic performance did not play a significant role as mediator in the processes that connect parent-teen relationships with depressive symptomatology. Even though GPA was by no means inconsequential to adolescent self-esteem, it was not established as a key variable in the development of depressed mood.

Hypothesis 10 is supported even though the relative mediation of scholastic performance was quite weak:

H10. Academic achievement should more powerfully mediate the relationship between dyadic parent-adolescent involvement and self-esteem than parental attachment and self-esteem.

Despite marginal levels of mediation, academic achievement was a stronger mediator in the relationship between paternal involvement and female adolescent self-esteem than either of the relationships between dyadic attachment and girls' self-esteem. For boys, scholastic success somewhat mediated maternal involvement and self-esteem outcomes, but did not affect attachment relations. Still, results support that parental involvement was more salient to the instrumental domain of adolescent academic achievement than was parental attachment. Findings advocate the importance of parental involvement in providing social capital for the facilitation children's successful cognitive development.

The final hypothesis of the cross-sectional analyses put forth the following:

H11. Adolescents' relationships with fathers should be more significant to academic outcomes than relationships with mothers.

On the whole, relationships with fathers produced more powerful direct association with adolescent academic achievement than relationships with mothers. Although neither involvement relationship was significantly associated with female academic achievement, father-daughter attachment was found to be more influential than mother-daughter attachment. In addition, the connection between father-daughter relationships, but not mother-daughter relationships, and girls' depressive as well as self-esteem outcomes was modestly mediated by adolescent GPA. For males, although both maternal relationship domains were marginally significant to scholastic performance, paternal involvement was the dyadic domain most significant to academic success (p<.01).

Findings generally substantiate McDonald's theories of social power and parental identification, which contend that children identify with the parent they see as having the most knowledge, ability, and control in a given situation (McDonald 1977, 1980). McDonald maintained that adolescents perceived fathers as possessing more power than mothers and, as a result, paternal power was most salient to children's, particularly daughters', behavioral outcomes.

In concluding that paternal relations were in fact most relevant to teenagers' scholastic achievement, I suggest that in the instrumental domain of education, children are more likely to attribute authority and competence to fathers than mothers. Sensibly, social power models should have transformed quite radically in the past decades as women have progressively accrued monetary and intellectual resources. Despite such shifts, however, gender status beliefs have remained very much intact. Men are still apt to be categorized as decisive, rational, and commanding while women are more likely to be labeled as deferential, emotional, and expressive (Marini 1990; Ridgeway 2001). In regard to academics, it seems children implement cultural stereotypes in conferring referent and legitimate power to fathers rather than mothers.

6.1.4. Control Variables

Developmental Age: While developmental theorists are surprisingly ambivalent as to the typical pathways that self-esteem follows through the course of adolescence, researchers tend to identify early adolescents as having the lowest self-esteem or claim that self-esteem remains relatively stable throughout the period (DuBois et al., 1998; Simmons et al., 1973; Savin-Williams & Demo, 1984). The longstanding developmental template is most likely to point toward early adolescence as the period of peak self-concept disturbance, mid-adolescence as a time in which teenagers become more socially and interpersonally secure, and late adolescence as the final solidification of those identities.

In contrast to academic assumptions of adolescent self-esteem formation, the present analysis found that, on average, middle adolescent females and late adolescent males actually had lower self-esteem and higher depressive affect than the youngest adolescents. Considering that the negotiation of autonomous identities is a gradual process, it is possible that any adverse effects to self-esteem would arise slowly as children detach from parents and face unprecedented interpersonal changes. Findings demonstrate that merging teenage boys and girls into one adolescent category is flawed since each sex experiences very unique developmental paths.

Overall, developmental age was a stronger predictor of adolescent male depression than adolescent female depression. On average, adolescent males were most depressed during late adolescence. Not surprising, boys' self-esteem was shown to follow a trajectory of deteriorating self-worth with adolescent age. Self-esteem powerfully mediated the effect of developmental age on adolescent male depressed mood. Longitudinal models established that adolescent males who were mid-adolescents at time 1 were at significantly greater risk for depression at time 2. Worsening psychological state seems to coincide with adolescent boys' detachment from parents. As relationships with parents become increasingly less significant to boys' affective states, risks for depression and self-esteem depletion escalated. As illustrated in interaction regressions, the linkage between father-son attachment and sons' self-esteem was most pronounced during early adolescence and least significant during late adolescence. It was late adolescence, when parent-child relationships were least salient, that represented the most troubling period for teenage boys.

For girls, mid-adolescence marked the period of highest depressive symptomatology and lowest self-esteem overall. In contrast to male peers, analyses suggest that girls' self-esteem rebounds during late adolescence. More specifically, regressions that interacted parent-daughter relationships on girls' developmental age demonstrated that both mother and father attachment were most significant to girls' self-esteem during the beginning of adolescent identity development (7th-8th grade). Moreover, maternal attachment was found to be more salient to early adolescent females than paternal attachment.

Even though boys and girls have gender specific psychosocial development, both are most impacted by same-sex parental attachment during the beginning of the adolescent period. Not surprisingly, it is during early adolescence that gender expectations are most heightened. The current analysis strengthens the belief that, for children experiencing gender-role intensification during early adolescence, relationships with same-sex parents become integral points of reference by which adolescents negotiate their own sense of selves as autonomous beings. Incorporating age-specific interactions highlighted the magnitude of mother-daughter and father-son relations during the beginning of the adolescent period.

For both males and females, having been held back in school was associated with greater risks for depression, deficient self-esteem, and lower school grades.

Parental Educational Attainment: In general, regressions strongly supported that higher levels of parental education were associated with lower levels of depression and higher academic achievement among children. Although both maternal and paternal education were important to adolescent psychological outcomes, findings pertaining to maternal education were more consistent. Mothers' increased educational attainment was found to be moderately tied to components of self-esteem for sons only while the educational attainment of both mothers and fathers was uniformly significant to children's academic outcomes. In fact, the linkage between teenagers' psychological states and the highest levels of parental education (e.g. college graduate, post college education) were mediated quite considerably by academic achievement. Thus, evidence provided herein suggests that high levels of parental education promote adolescent academic achievement.

In conclusion, my prediction that educational attainment of same-sex parents would be most significant to adolescents' emotional outcomes was contested. The lack of significance reported in the educational attainment and adolescent self-esteem relationship suggests that parent-adolescent relationship dyads absorb a portion of this potential influence.

Findings also challenge social power theories of parental identification that expect fathers to represent legitimate power within families and, thus, more significantly impact children's instrumental activities, such as scholastic performance (Scanzoni 1991; Starrels 1992). However, given that paternal attachment was found to be more salient to teenage female academic achievement than maternal attachment, I do not entirely reject social power theories.

Maternal Employment Status: Although mother's employment status was unrelated to adolescent male psychosocial and cognitive outcomes, daughters with employed mothers were marginally more likely to be depressed than daughters with stay-at-home mothers. However, reports indicate that self-esteem did not mediate the relationship between maternal employment status and depressive symptoms. The fact that maternal employment was found to have little bearing on female adolescent self-concepts suggests other reasons for increased risk for depression. Even though the present analysis cannot account for employment satisfaction or even occupation, it is nevertheless important to recognize that a mother's job dissatisfaction or heightened levels of daily stress have been associated with poor child well-being (Burchinal & Rossman 1961; Pett et al. 1994).

In accordance with social capital models, the negative effects of mothers working outside the home may be associated with decreased accessibility (Coleman 1988). In opposition to studies that have cited negative consequences for sons of working mothers (Booth & Amato 1994), the present analysis finds no association between maternal work status and sons' emotional health. Overall, the relatively weak results suggest that most of the impact, whether positive or negative, of mother's work status is absorbed by mother-child relationships and maternal education.

Adolescent Race-Ethnicity: Racial-ethnic status proved to be a chief determinant of teenagers' emotional and cognitive outcomes. The present investigation's results are consistent with past studies that have asserted significantly higher self-esteem among

Black adolescents as compared to adolescents of other races (Hughes & Demo, 1989; Rotheram-Borus et al., 1996). However, despite enhanced self-esteem, non-Hispanic Black females were not found to be protected from depressive risks. As expected, self-esteem did not appear to be a source of depression for Black girls, but rather depressive symptomatology seemed to develop as a result of other factors. One source of increased depressive symptoms and decreased self-esteem appeared to be academic achievement, which was significantly lower among the female sample's Black teens as compared to White teens.

On the other hand, Black males were not appreciably more or less depressed than White males. However, African American males did have, on average, significantly lower school grades than White peers, which worked to decrease self-esteem despite the fact that Black male self-esteem was, overall, considerably higher than the self-esteem of males of all other racial categories.

Also significant were findings that non-Hispanic Asian American adolescents had, on average, greater psychosocial disturbance and lower self-esteem than adolescents of other racial categories. Not surprisingly, low self-esteem played a strong mediating role in the development of depressed mood. In contrast, academic achievement, which was highest among Asian respondents, improved emotional well-being somewhat. Though it is beyond the scope of this particular examination, studies of adolescent self-esteem would benefit from deeper analysis of cultural implications that seem to impair Asian adolescents' psychological health.

The lack of noteworthy findings regarding immigrant status failed to corroborate Harker's 2001 study that reported significantly lower depressive symptoms in first-generation immigrants as compared to native peers. The present investigation found that immigrants had neither lower nor higher depressed mood, self-esteem, or school grades than native classmates.

Adolescent Religiosity: Despite the fact that one regression model illustrated that very religious females were significantly more like to be depressed than females who were not religious, religious beliefs were not found to be particularly significant to depressive outcomes overall. However, the consistent significant link between religiosity and higher female self-esteem supports the contention that spiritual beliefs facilitate positive self-concepts (Miller and Merav 2002; Schapman & Inderbitzen 2002). Religion seems to be beneficial to girls, who are socialized to value emotional attributes. Utilizing the concept of psychological centrality, the greater import an adolescent girl places on religion, the more central religion should be to her identity. As a result, religiosity should hold great psychological significance.

Strangely enough, while cross-sectional models showed no significant relationship between religiosity and adolescent male psychosocial outcomes, longitudinal models revealed positive long-term effects for religious males. Compared to nonreligious males, boys who held religious beliefs at time 1 had significantly higher self-esteem and lower depressive affect at time 2. Furthermore, increased religiosity was found to be positively associated with male and female academic achievement, although association was more powerful for girls.

As a whole, predictions that religiosity would be linked more strongly to female psychosocial health due to females' tendency to place more emphasis on emotional support was not upheld once longitudinal models were taken into account. What is clear is that, regardless of adolescent gender, religion was found to be an essential aspect of self-concept for youth who possess such beliefs.

Sibling Composition: While male adolescents who had one or two siblings were found to be moderately more depressed than only children, boys with four or more siblings had significantly higher self-esteem than those who were only children. Findings discount the Resource Dilution hypothesis, which abides by the premise that additional siblings diminish parental attention available (Hofferth et al. 1988). If social capital were truly diluted by additional siblings then respondents with three or four siblings should be at greatest risk for mood disturbance, lower self-worth, and poor scholastic performance (Downey 1995; Steelman et al. 2002). This, in fact, was not the case. Sibling composition was not related to adolescent academic achievement nor was it related to females' emotional or cognitive well-being.

Sexual Relations: Cross-sectional and longitudinal analyses presented contradictory findings in regard to sexual activity. In cross-sectional models, sexually active adolescents had significantly higher mood disturbance and lower grade point averages than virgin peers. Romantic sex, in particular, was linked to higher depressed mood for females but lower depressed mood for males. In these models, sexual activity was, for the most part, unrelated to teens' self-esteem. Only virgins who had nonromantic sexual relations were at greater risk for poor self-worth than virgins.

However, longitudinal models displayed that various types of time 1 sexual activity actually promoted self-esteem, especially for boys. Longitudinal regressions found that females who had experienced romantic as well as nonromantic sexual relations at time 1 had higher self-esteem at Wave 2. Boys who initially stated to have had either romantic or nonromantic sex had higher self-esteem one year later. Problematic, however, was that models did not account for sexual activity experienced between interviews. Given that adolescence marks a period of sexual exploration for many teens, this weakens the results significantly.

The cross-sectional findings partially correspond to Joyner and Udry's 2001 study that found correlation between romantic relationships and higher rates of depressive affect for male and female adolescents. In the present study, however, romantic relations emerged as damaging to girls' depressive outcomes but beneficial to boys' psychological health. In accordance with theories of gender socialization, I contend that the significance of intimate connections to female self-concepts makes the acquisition and maintenance of romantic partners exceedingly psychologically central to self-worth (Dyk & Adams 1990; Gilligan 1996). Since boys tend to be less personally invested in romantic relations than girls, the effects of relationship dysfunction or dissolution should be far more traumatic for girls. Nevertheless, both male and female virgins were, on average, less depressed than sexually active peers.

Findings related to rape were relatively surprising. For females, having been a victim of rape heightened depressed mood, but was not significantly associated with self-esteem or academic achievement. According to this analysis, rape engenders depressive symptomatology but does not wound girls' sense of selves. For males, longitudinal analyses found that respondents who had perpetrated rape at time 1 were at considerable risk for depression at time 2. This finding suggests that rapists do eventually suffer emotional repercussions for their crimes.

Extracurricular Participation: Overall, involvement in extracurricular activities emerged as beneficial to adolescent emotional and cognitive well-being. For example, club membership, but not athletic status, was related to higher academic grades. Granted, cross-sectional methods present an issue of causation in which students with high grades may join clubs in pursuit of intellectual development or in order to strengthen college applications. Therefore, one should be cautioned not to infer causality as it pertains to the aforementioned cognitive outcome.

Although participation associated with athletics enhanced self-esteem and protected teenage males from depression, it was not significantly associated with adolescent females' emotional outcomes. Subsequent longitudinal findings confirmed that athletic participation, whether combined with club membership or not, bolstered self-esteem for males. Yet, longitudinal regressions revealed causal relationships between girls' participation in clubs and sports, which were found to instigate lower and higher depressive symptoms, respectively, over time.

As a whole, results showed that extracurricular activities provided teenagers with a constructive venue for psychosocial development (Anderman 2002; Eccles et al. 2001 Maton 1990). Findings also support that male athletes obtained highly esteemed masculine status, which suited their achievement-orientations and facilitated positive identities (Eccles et al. 1987; Hill & Lynch 1983; Shanahan et al. 1991). In the current analysis, the potential negative effects of high school sports involvement were only experienced by teenage females. It is possible that girls, who are raised to value camaraderie and acquiescence, suffer stress and anxiety related to competition (Smoll & Smith 1996; Eccles & Barber 1999; Eder & Parker 1987).

Quality of Friendships: Undoubtedly, relationships with same-aged peers are essential to adolescent psychosocial well-being. In concurrence with predictions, friendships were found to impact teens' psychological components of depressed mood and self-esteem, but not scholastic outcomes. Findings suggest that friends represent valuable sources of interpersonal connection, mutual understanding, and companionship (Adler & Adler 1998; Bukowski et al. 1993; Hartup 1993; Lansford et al. 2003). Particularly for interdependent females, it is believed that friends become trustworthy confidants who impart secure intimate connections so important for self-concept definition (Youniss & Smollar 1985).

Adolescent Body Weight: Overweight status adversely affected adolescent academic performance and self-esteem, particularly for female adolescents. Although being overweight was found to increase risks for depression among males, it did not generate depressive risks for girls until the longitudinal model was introduced.

Results were fairly surprising for a number of reasons. First, no significance emerged in regard to underweight status. The fact that the weight variable was operationalized through teenagers' self-reports could have compromised the analysis. For instance, girls who were most concerned with body image may have been inclined to exaggerate weight if they had an eating disorder or underreport weight if they were heavier than other peers. Second, the significant relationship exhibited between overweight status and academic performance was unexpected. The linkage is disconcerting as it may signify that adolescents are relinquishing attempts for healthier minds and bodies collectively. Finally, the causal influence of overweight status to worsening self-esteem in males, but not females, was unforeseen. Clearly, the repercussions of overweight status do not only impact girls. In fact, boys demonstrated significant self-concept disturbance as a result of being overweight. Considering the present day epidemic in which American children and adolescents face unprecedented rates of obesity, the association between adolescent overweight status and negative psychosocial and cognitive outcomes is revealing.

6.2. Longitudinal Analysis

In longitudinal regressions, the first hypothesis was supported while the latter two were generally rejected.

H1. Time 1 adolescent depressed mood, adolescent self-esteem, parental attachment, and parental involvement variables should be significantly and positively associated with corresponding time 2 variables, thereby indicating stability over time.

H2. Time 1 parent-adolescent relationship domains, controlling for time 1 depressed mood, should be inversely associated with adolescent depressed mood at time 2.

H3. Time 1 parent-adolescent relationship domains, controlling for time 1 self-esteem, should be positively associated with adolescent self-esteem at time 2.

The fact that all primary time 1 variables were highly correlated with time 2 counterparts substantiates Hypothesis 1. More important, findings suggest that adolescence itself is not a period of unhinged social turmoil and erratic emotions, but is rather a far more stable developmental period.

In contrast to the predictions of hypothesis 2, of all eight dyadic relationship domain pairings, only father-daughter attachment produced causal association with adolescent depressed mood. I suggest that a fundamental reason for the overall lack of results is due to the stability of adolescent depressive state from time 1 to time 2. Given that depression develops gradually as a process of psychological deterioration, the fact that only one year transpired between assessments could have impaired the methodological facility of the longitudinal regression analyses. Still, the significance of father-daughter attachment only further supports the importance of fathers to daughters' psychosocial well-being.

Hypothesis 3 was partially supported through longitudinal analyses. Although no involvement relationships demonstrated causal association with adolescent self-esteem, all dyadic parent-teen attachment relations predicted time 2 adolescent self-esteem. Since age-graded changes to self-esteem tend to be more pronounced than changes to depressive state, it is sensible that causal effects emerged over the relatively short span of time. Although each dyadic attachment relationship was significant at the $p<.01$ level, mothers and fathers similarly influenced daughters' self-esteem while mothers were stronger predictors of male adolescent self-esteem than attachment with fathers.

One of the most telling findings of longitudinal analyses found that depressed mood contributed to worsening self-esteem over time for boys but not girls. This gender-specific finding suggests that cultural stereotypes that consider negative depressive states to be weak for male identities may be acutely damaging to male self-esteem.

CHAPTER SEVEN
CONCLUSION

7.1. Limitations

Several weaknesses of this investigation should be recognized and clarified. Despite the fact that longitudinal methods enable readers to infer causality between parent-child relationship quality and adolescent psychosocial well-being, some shortcomings should be noted. First, the timeframe between Wave 1 and Wave 2 was only one year. Given the short period of time between interviews, the changes to adolescents' emotional states were not, nor should they have been, considerable. Future studies that investigate adolescent health using multiple waves with longer windows of time between interviews appear warranted.

As corroborated by the present investigation, adolescence is now considered to be a more stable period than previously thought. Longitudinal analyses demonstrate that time 1 adolescent depressed mood, adolescent self-esteem, and dyadic parent-teen relationship domains were highly correlated with respective time 2 counterparts. Thus, for those adolescents who do suffer emotional disturbance, the fact that processes leading to self-concept disturbance and depressive symptomatology are gradual is beneficial since parents, educators, and physicians have ample opportunity to intervene and prevent further deterioration of adolescent psychosocial functioning. Further, the strong correlative power of all dyadic parent-adolescent pairings discounts notions of adolescence as a time of intense parent-child conflict and relationship corrosion. Instead, findings suggest that most adolescents remain close to and continue to identify with parents throughout the period

Secondly, due to the fact that self-esteem is ultimately shaped by one's own views, adolescent perceptions were used to measure each parent-teen relationship domain. Problematic however is the potential for "halo effects", in which a child's relationship with one parent influences his or her relationship with the other parent (Acock & Yang 1984; Boyd 1989). As shown in bivariate correlations, relationships with mothers and fathers were significantly associated (Table 1). Nevertheless, the mean differences found in mother-adolescent and father-adolescent relationship domains do suggest that such adverse effects were not a major concern within this particular analysis.

Third, these data do not allow for the assessment of parental depression. Literature contends that children with depressed parents are predisposed to depressive disorders by way of both genetic and behavioral risk factors (Pike and Plomin 1996; Shaffer et al. 1996; Warner et al. 1999). Future studies that control for parental depressive state would offer a more comprehensive evaluation of familial history risks.

Finally, in examining sources of adolescent self-esteem, this book focused on adolescent gender rather than gender identity. A number of studies have found direct association between children's level of masculinity or femininity and emotional competency (Burke 1989; Marsh 1987; Whitley 1983). In fact, Renk and Creasey (2003) determined that adolescent coping strategies were more indicative of adolescent gender identity than gender itself. If possible, future analyses should incorporate explanatory variables that measure gender as well as gender identity.

7.2. Conclusion

The complexity of the processes that lead to depressed mood calls for meticulous attention to adolescent relations with both parents as well as adolescent gender. The primary aim of this investigation was to better understand the effects of dyadic parent-teen attachment and involvement on adolescent male and female depressed mood and, further, to explore the mediating effects of adolescent self-esteem and academic achievement within the primary relationship. While self-esteem proved to be a fundamental component of the development of depressed mood, the mediating effects of academic achievement were relatively weak. Still, the current analysis corroborates that self-esteem plays a central role in the development of depressive symptoms, particularly for female teens.

This book offers a better understanding of how same-sex and cross-sex parent-teen relationships impact self-esteem and mood disturbance during the pivotal period in which adolescents form self-concepts and build emotional foundations needed to face the challenges of adolescence and ultimately adulthood. Findings that highlight the significance of parent-adolescent gender dyads to the development of healthy minds are important to social psychological research.

Results coincide with current literature in finding that girls faced considerably higher depressive risks than boys. While self-esteem proved to be a strong mediator in the processes that led to depressed mood for both adolescent males and females, females were found to be more susceptible to depression-inducing self-esteem depletion. The present investigation emphasizes the consequences of socialization that differentiate children along clear gender lines. Socially constructed gender expectations clearly impact boys' and girls' behavior and values in profound and undeniable ways. Unless research becomes more focused on the critical role of gender and gender socialization in shaping sources of self-esteem, girls who embark upon adolescence less prepared than their male counterparts will continue to suffer higher rates of depression and emotional disadvantages throughout their lives. This study underscores adolescent girls' sensitivity to relationship-oriented influences in their psychosocial development of selves. However, in such an endeavor researchers must be cautious not to neglect adolescent boys and their need for positive self-esteem. As substantiated throughout this manuscript, adolescent females' vulnerability to psychological impairment should not undermine the perceptible risks faced by adolescent males.

A key conclusion of this book highlights the influence of adolescent gender and developmental age to the processes that lead to depressive symptomatology. Despite the fact that boys and girls follow gender-specific developmental trajectories, both are shown to be most impacted by same-sex parental attachment during the beginning of the adolescent period. Not surprisingly, it is during early adolescence that gender expectations are most heightened. For children experiencing gender-role intensification during early adolescence, it seems that relationships with same-sex parents become integral points of reference by which children negotiate their sense of selves as autonomous beings.

Not surprising, the most salient of all dyadic pairings was found to be that of mothers and daughters. However, while results confirming the importance of same-sex parent-child relationships correspond with the majority of available research, findings that highlight the salience of cross-sex relations to adolescent psychological health conflict with prevailing philosophy. For example, the importance of teenage girls' relations with fathers debunks beliefs that father-daughter relationships are void of emotional and physical connection (Dornbusch 1989; Steinberg 1987). Clearly, girls' dependency on emotional attachment and appraisals reflected from both parents promotes positive self-concepts and insulates girls from depressive risks. Findings presented in this book concur with theories of gender socialization and gender identity expectations, which maintain that girls are socialized to value and define themselves through intimate connections with significant others. Furthermore, the significance of mother-son relations, particularly pertaining to self-esteem, exemplifies the importance of mothers to sons' affective components of well-being.

Much can be done to help those adolescents at risk for or already suffering from depression. For example, federal and school initiatives should advocate education that raises awareness in matters of depression for students as well as those individuals most involved in teens' lives, such as parents, teachers, coaches, and peers. Educational institutions should organize mandatory meetings for school employees and students in which health professionals train those individuals to recognize possible symptoms of depression. Furthermore, as exhibited throughout this book, since depressed mood is manifested in different ways by girls and boys, the implications of gender on depression should be clarified. The present analysis, which illustrates the salience of friendships during adolescence, suggests that peers can be invaluable in identifying students in need of help. At-risk adolescents cannot suffer as schools become increasingly large and impersonal.

Proper diagnosis is critical to effective treatment and recovery of depression. Despite increased awareness of teenage depression, as recently as 2001 the National Institute of Mental Health estimated that over seventy percent of child and adolescent depressive disorders were misdiagnosed or mistreated (Bhatia & Bhatia 2007). Accurate diagnosis requires multi-level assessment. First, credible surveys that assess teens' self-esteem and depressive affect, such as those used in the current study, may be useful in identifying those students in need of intervention. Every school should staff an appropriate number of qualified mental health professionals or certified clinical social workers to counsel those students susceptible to, or suffering from, depression. Whether in-house or not, psychologists or psychiatrists who have the ability to accurately diagnose and treat depression should be accessible to students. For mild to moderate depressive states, cognitive behavior therapy may be most appropriate while psychiatric treatment may be necessary for severe recurrent depression (Bhatia & Bhatia 2007). Comprehensive treatment plans should include individual adolescent and parent as well as conjoint family therapy that stress the healing of selves and relationships. If parents cannot or refuse to support their children, caring same-sex adult figures should be assigned to establish enduring relations with at-risk adolescents. Trained and screened representatives could be volunteers or hired associates, and might include relatives, coaches, spiritual advisors, counselors, or adults who overcame depression themselves. Mentors can convey to depressed adolescents how much they matter to others and instill in them a sense of personal agency, promote optimism for productive and happy futures, and encourage positive self-views. One cannot underestimate the importance of early detection and treatment of adolescent depression. Federal mandates should ensure that insurance covers all psychotherapy and counseling costs. After all, depression is a credible mental illness and if untreated can lead to enduring harm, possibly even suicide.

As shown throughout this book, parents are critically significant to adolescents' psychosocial health and, therefore, should play active roles in prevention strategies. Mailings may be a particularly useful and cost-effective way to educate parents about adolescent depression. Guide books or brochures that clearly and concisely outline the prevalence, warning signs, and consequences of teenage depression can offer suggestions as to how best to deal with depression in order to better inform parents on the subject. For example, a campaign sponsored by the Boston Coalition for Children and Adolescent Mental Health provides brochures to parents and teens, which include referrals for online, phone, and local support services. Despite their children's need for autonomy and increased time spent with peers, parents should be aware of the continued importance of secure homes and warm, caring, and communicative parent-adolescent relationships, particularly among same-sex dyads.

While it is impractical, though not impossible to transform deeply entrenched social structures, current goals should ultimately seek to promote healthy adolescent psychosocial development amid such gendered forces. Although the journey through adolescence may be inevitably challenging, the voyage through it can and should be eased. Recognizing that sources of adolescent depressed mood differ considerably by adolescent gender will help parents, teachers, and researchers gain valuable knowledge of the development of adolescent selves.

REFERENCES

Acock, A.C. & Yang, W. S. (1984). Parental power and adolescents' parental identification. *Journal of Marriage and the Family, 46*, 487-495.

Adler, P. & Adler, P. (1998). *Peer power: Preadolescent culture and identity*. New Brunswick, NJ: Rutgers University Press.

Ainsworth, M., Blehar M.C., Waters E., & Wall, S. (1978). *Patterns of Attachment*. Hillsdale, NJ: Erlbaum.

Alasker, F., & Olweus, D. (1992). Stability of global self-evaluation in early adolescence: A cohort longitudinal study. *Journal of Research on Adolescence, 1*, 123-145.

Amato, P. R. (1986). Marital conflict, the parent-child relationship and child self-esteem. *Family Relations, 35*(3), 403-410.

Amato, P. R. (1994). Father-child relations, mother-child relations, and offspring psychological well-being in early adulthood. *Journal of Marriage and the Family* 56, 1031-1042.

Anderman, E. M. (2002). School effects on psychological outcomes during adolescence. *American Psychological Association, 94*(4), 795-809.

Anderson, R. N. (2002). *Deaths: Leading causes for 2000. National Vital Statistics Reports,* 50, National Center for Health Statistics.

Angold, A., Costello, E. J., Erkanli, A., & Worthman, C. M. (1999). Pubertal changes in hormone levels and depression in girls. *Psychological Medicine, 29*, 1043-1053.

Armsden, G. C., McCauley E., Greenberg, M. T., Burke, M. T., & Mitchell, J. R. (1990). Parent and peer attachment in early adolescent depression. *Journal of Abnormal Psychology, 18*, 683-697.

Arnett, J. J. (1999). Adolescent storm and stress. *American Psychologist, 54*(5), 317-326.

Arnett, J. J. (2000). Emerging adulthood: A theory of development from the late teens through the twenties. *American Psychologist,* 57, 774-783.

Astone, N. M., McLanahan, S. S. (1991). Family Structure, Parental Practices and High-School Completion. *American Sociological Review*, 56(3), 309-320.

Attie, I. & Brooks-Gunn, J. (1989). Development of eating problems in adolescent girls. *Developmental Psychology,* 25, 70-79.

Avenevoli, S. & Steinberg, L. (2000). The continuity of depression across the adolescent transition. In H. Reese & R. Kail (Ed.), *Advances in Child Development and Behvavior*.

Avison, W. R., & McAlpine, D. D. (1992). Gender differences and symptoms of depression among adolescents. *Journal of Health and Social Behavior, 33*, 77-96.

Baltes, M. M., & Silverberg, S. (1994). The dynamics between dependency and autonomy: illustrations across the lifespan. In D. L. Featherman, Lerner, R. M. and Perlmutter, M. (Ed.), *Life-Span Development and Behaviour* (Vol. 12, pp. 41-90). Hillsdale, NJ: Lawrence Erlbaum.

Bandura, A. (2001). Social Cognitive Theory: An Agentic Perspective. *Annual Review of Psychology, 52*, 1-26.

Bandura, A., & Walters, R. (1959). *Adolescent Aggression*. New York: Ronald Press.

Bandura, A. (1986). *Social Foundations of Thought and Action: A Social Cognitive Theory*. Englewood Cliffs, NJ: Prentice Hall.

Bandura, A., Barbaranelli, C., Vittrio, G., & Pastorelli, C. (1996). Multi-faceted impact of self-efficacy beliefs on academic functioning. *Child Development, 67*(3), 1206-1222.

Bandura, A., Pastorelli, C., Barbaranelli, C., & Caprara, G. V. (1999). Self-efficacy pathways to childhood depression. *Journal of Personality and Social Psychology, 76*, 258-269.

Bandura, A., Ross, D., & Ross, S. (1963). A comparative test of status envy, social power and secondary reinforcement theories of identifcation. *Journal of Abnormal and Social Psychology, 67*, 527-534.

Barber, B. L. (1994). Support and advice from married and divorced fathers. *Family Relations, 43*, 433-438.

Barber, B. L., & Thomas, D. L. (1986). Dimensions of fathers' and mothers' supportive behavior: The case for physical affection. *Journal of Marriage and the Family* 48, 783-794.

Barber, J. G., & Delfabbro, P. (2000). Predictors of adolescent adjustment: Parent-peer relationships and parent-child conflict. *Child and Adolescent Social Work Journal, 17*(4), 275-288.

Barber, B. K., & Olsen, J. A. (2004). Assessing the transitions to middle and high school. *Journal of Adolescent Research, 19*(1), 3-30.

Baumeister, R. F., Campbell, J. D., Krueger, J. I., & Vohs, K. D. (2003). Does high self-esteem cause better performance, interpersonal success, happiness, or healthier lifestyles? *Psychological Science in the Public Interest, 4*(1), 1-44.

Beck, A. T. (1967). *Depression: Clinical, experimental, and theoretical aspects*. New York: Harper & Row.

Bem, D. J. (1967). Self-perception: An alternative interpretation of cognitive dissonance phenomena. *Psychological Review*, 74, 183–200.

Ben-Zur, H. (2003). Happy adolescents: The link between subjective well-being, internal resources, and parental factors. *Journal of Youth and Adolescence, 32*(2), 67-79.

Betz, N. E., & Klein, K. L. (1996). Relationships among measures of career self-efficacy, generalized self-efficacy, and global self-esteem. *Journal of Career Assessment, 4*, 285-298.

Beutel, A. M., & Marini, M. M. (1995). Gender and values. *American Sociological Review, 60*, 436-448.

Bhatia, S. K., & Bhatia, S. C. (2007). Childhood and Adolescent Depression. *American Family Physician,* 75, 73-80.

Bianchi, S. M., & Robinson, J. (1997). What did you do today? Children's use of time, family composition, and the acquisition of social capital. *Journal of Marriage and the Family,* 59(2), 332-344.

Black, K. A. (2002). Associations between adolescent-mother and adolescent-best friend interactions. *Adolescence, 37*(146), 235-254.

Blake, J. (1981). Family Size and the Quality of Children. *Demography,* 18, 421-442.

Blake, J. (1985). Number of Siblings and Educational Mobility. *American Sociological Review*, 50, 84-94.

Blos, P. (1985). *Son and Father: Before and Beyond the Oedipus Complex*. New York: The Free Press.

Blyth, D., Simmons, R. G., & Bush, D. (1978). The transition into early adolescence: A longitudinal comparison of youth in two educational contexts. *Sociology of Education,* 51, 149-162.

Bogenschneider, K., Wu, M. Raffaelli M., & Tsay, J.C. (1998). Parent influences on adolescent peer orientation and substance sue: The interface of parenting practices and values. *Child Development,* 69, 1672-1688

Bohan, J. S. (1973). Age and sex differences in self-concept. *Adolescence, VIII*(31), 379-384.

Bonney, J. F., Kelley, M. L., & Levant, R. F. (1999). A model of fathers' involvement in child care in dual-earner families. *Journal of Family Psychology, 13*(3), 401-415.

Bordo, S. (1993). *Unbearable Weight*. Berkeley, CA: University of California Press.

Bowlby, J. (1958). The nature of a child's tie to his mother. *International Journal of Psycho-Analysis, 39*, 350-373.

Bowlby, J. (1973). *Attachment and Loss, 2: Separation, Anxiety and Anger*. New York: Basic Books.

Bowlby, J. (1980). *Attachment and Loss, 3: Loss, Sadness and Depression*. New York: Basic Books.

Boyd, C. J. (1989). Mothers and daughters: A discussion of theory and research. *Journal of Marriage and the Family, 51*, 291-301.

Brage, D., Campbell-Grossman, C., & Dunkel, J. (1995). Psychological correlates of adolescent depression. *Journal of Child and Adolescent Psychiatric Nursing, 8*, 23-30.

Brent D.A., Johnson, B.A., Perper J., Connolly J., Bridge J., Bartle S., & Rather C. (1994). Personality disorder, personality traits, impulsive violence, and completed suicide in adolescents. *Journal of the American Academy of Child and Adolescent Psychiatry*, 33(8), 1080-1086.

Bretherton, I. (1994). The Origins of Attachment Theory: John Bowlby and Mary Ainsworth. In R. D. Parke, Peter Ornstein, John Rieser, and Carolyn Zahn-Waxler (Ed.), *A Century of Developmental Psychology*. Washington D.C.: American Psychological Association.

Bronfenbrenner, U. (1979). The ecology of human development: Experiments by nature and design. Cambridge, MA: Harvard University Press.

Brooks-Gunn, J & Warren, M. P. (1989). Biological and social contributions to negative affect in young adolescent girls. *Child Development, 60*, 40-55.

Brown, B. B. (1990). Peer Groups and Peer Cultures. In S. S. Feldman & G. R. Elliott (Eds.), *At the Threshold: The Developing Adolescent* (pp. 171-196). Cambridge, MA: Harvard University Press.

Brown, B. B., & Lohr, M. J. (1987). Peer group affiliation and adolescent self-esteem: An integration of ego-identity and symbolic interaction theories. *Journal of Personal Social Psychology*, 52, 47-55.

Brown, G. W. & Harris, T. O. (1978) *Social Origins of Depression: A Study of Psychiatric Disorder in Women.* London: Tavistock.

Brown, K. M., McMahon, R. P., Biro, F. M., Crawford, P., Schreibner, G. B., Similo, S. L., Waclawiw, M., & Striegel-Moore, R. (1998). Changes in self-esteem among black and white girls between the ages of 9 and 14 years. *Journal of Adolescent Health,* 23, 7-19.

Buist, K., Dekovic, M., Meeus, W., & Van Aken, M. A. G. (2002). Developmental patterns in adolescent attachment to mother, father, and sibling. *Journal of Youth and Adolescence* 31, no. 3, 167-176.

Bukowski, W., Hoza, B., & Boivin, M. (1993). Popularity, Friendship, and Emotional Adjustment During Early Adolescence. In B. Laursen (Ed.), *New Directions for Child Development: Close Friendships in Adolescence* (Vol. 60, pp. 23-37). San Francisco: Jossey-Bass Publishers.

Burchinal, L. G., & Rossman, J. E. (1961). Relations among maternal employment indices and developmental characteristics of children. *Marriage and Family Living,* 334-340.

Burke, P. J. (1989). Gender Identity, Sex, and School Performance. *Social Psychological Quarterly,* 52(2), 159-169.

Burke, P. J. (1996). Psycho-social stress: Perspectives on structure, theory, life-course, and methods. In H. B. Kaplan (Ed.), *Social identities and psycho-social stress* (Vol. 1). San Diego: Academic Press.

Bussey, K. & Bandura A. (1999). Social cognitive theory of gender development and differentiation. *Psychological Review,* 106, 676-713.

Cabrera, N. J., Tamis-LeMonda C. S., Bradley, R. H., Hofferth, S., & M. E. Lamb, M. E. (2000). Fatherhood in the twenty-first century. *Child Development* 71(1), 127-136.

Call, K. T., Riedel, A. A., Hein, K., McLoyd, V., Petersen, A., & Kipke, M. (2002). Adolescent health and well-being in the twenty-first century: A global perspective. *Journal of Research on Adolescence,* 12(1), 69-98.

Carlson, G. A., & Cantwell, D. P. (1982). Suicidal behavior and depression in children and adolescents. *Journal of the American Academy of Child Adolescent Psychiatry,* 21, 361-368.

Carlson, C., Uppal, S., & Prosser, E. C. (2000). Ethnic differences in processes contributing to the self-esteem of early adolescent girls. *Journal of Early Adolescence,* 20(1), 44-59.

Casper, R. C. & Offer, D. (1990). Weight and dieting concerns in adolescents: Fashion of Symptom? *Pediatrics,* 86, 384-390.

Cast, A., & Burke, P. (2002). A Theory of Self-Esteem. *Social Forces, 8-,* 1041-1068.

Centers for Disease Control and Prevention. (1999). http://www.cdc.gov/ncipc/factsheets/suifacts.htm.

Centers for Disease Control and Prevention. (2002). *Prevalence of overweight and obese among adults: 1999-2002.* http://www.cdc.gov/nchs/products/pubs/pubd/hestats/obese/obese99.htm.

Centers for Disease Control and Prevention. (2003). National Center for Chronic Disease Prevention and Health Promotion, Youth Risk Behavior Survey.

Center for Mental Health Services. (1998). http://www.mentalhealth.samhsa.gov/cmhs/MentalHealthStatistics.

Cheng, H. & Furnham, A. (2003). Personality, self-esteem, and demographic predictions of happiness and depression. *Personality and Individual Differences,* 34, 921-942.

Chodorow, N. (1974). "Family Structure and the Feminine Personality." In M. Z. Rosaldo & L. Lamphere (Ed.), *Women, Culture and Society.* Stanford, CA: Stanford University Press.

Chodorow, N. (1978). *The Reproduction of Mothering.* Berkeley & LA: University of California Press.

Chubb, N. H, & Fertman, C. I. (1997). Adolescent self-esteem and locus of control: A longitudinal study of gender and age differences. *Adolescence, 32*(125), 113-125.

Clausen, J. (1991). Adolescent competence and the shaping of the life course. *American Journal of Sociology,* 96, 4-14.

Cohen, D. A., & Rice, J. (1997). Parenting styles, adolescent substance use, and academic achievement. *Journal of Drug Education, 27*(2), 199-211.

Colarossi, L. G., & Eccles, J. S. (2000). A prospective study of adolescents' peer support: Gender differences and the influence of parental relationships. *Journal of Youth and Adolescence, 29*(6), 661-678.

Coleman, J. (1961). The Adolescent Society: The Social Life of a Teenager and its impact on education. New York: The Free Press of Glencoe.

Coleman, J. (1988). Social capital and the creation of human capital. *American Journal of*

Sociology, 94 (supplement), 95-120.

Cooley, C. H. (1902). *Human nature and the social order.* New York: Charles Scribner's Sons.

Crockenberg, S., Jackson, S., & Langrock, A. M. (1996). Autonomy and goal attainment: Parenting, gender, and children's social competence. In M. Killen (Ed.). *Children's autonomy, social competence, and interactions with adults and other children: Exploring connections and consequences, 73,* 41-56. San Francisco: Jossey-Bass Publishers.

Crocker, J. & Luhtanen, R. K. (2003). Level of self-esteem and contingencies of self-worth: Unique effects on academic, social, and financial problems in college students. *Personality and Social Psychology Bulletin, 29,* 701-712.

Crockett, L. J., Petersen, A. C., Graber, J. A., Schulenberg, J. E., & Ebata, A. (1989). School transitions and adjustment during early adolescence. *Journal of Early Adolescence, 9,* 181-210.

Crosnoe, R., & Muller, C. (2004). Body mass index, academic achievement, and school context: Examining the educational experiences of adolescents at risk of obesity. *Journal of Health and Social Behavior, 45*(December), 393-407.

Cross, S. E., & Madson, L. (1997). Models of self-construals and gender. *Psychological Bulletin, 122*(1), 5-37.

Deaux, K. (1984). From Individual Differences to Social Categories. *American Psychologist, 39*(2), 105-116.

Deihl, L. M., Vicary J. R., & Deike, R. C. (1997). Longitudinal trajectories of self-esteem from early to middle adolescence and related psychosocial variables among rural adolescents. *Journal of Research on Adolescence, 7,* 393-411.

Demo, D. H., & Savin-Williams, R. C. (1983). Early adolescent self-esteem as a function of social class: Rosenberg and Pearlin revisited. *American Journal of Sociology, 88*(4), 763-774.

Demo, D. H., Small, S., & Savin-Williams, R. C. (1987). Family relations and the self-esteem of adolescents and their parents. *Journal of Marriage and the Family, 49,* 705-715.

Dornbusch, S. M., Carlsmith, J. M., Duncan, P. D., Gross, R. T., Martin, J. A., Ritter, P. L., & Siegel-Gorelik, B. (1984). Sexual maturation, social class, and the desire to be thin among adolescent females. *Developmental and Behavioral Pediatrics, 5,* 308-314.

Dornbusch, S. M., Ritter, P. L., Leiderman, P. O., Roberts, D. F., & Fraleigh, M. J. (1987). The relation of parenting style to adolescent school performance. *Child Development, 58,* 1244-1257.

Dornbusch, S. M. (1989). The sociology of adolescence. *Annual Review of Sociology, 15,* 233-259.

Downey, D. (1995). When Bigger is not Better: Family Size, Parental Resources, and Children's Educational Performance. *American Sociological Review, 60,* 746-761.

DuBois, D. L., Bull, C. A., Sherman, M. D., & Roberts, M. (1998). Self-esteem and adjustment in early adolescence: A social-contextual perspective. *Journal of Youth and Adolescence, 27*(5), 557-583.

Durkheim, E. (1915, 1947). *The Elementary Forms of Religious Life.* NY: Free Press.

Dworkin, J. B., Larson R., & Hansen, D. (2003). Adolescents' accounts of growth experiences in youth activities. *Journal of Youth and Adolescence, 32,* 17-26.

Dyk, P. H., & Adams, G. R. (1990). Identity and Intimacy: An initial investigation of three theoretical models using cross-lag panel correlations. *Journal of Youth and Adolescence, 19,* 91-110.

Eccles, J., & Barber, B. (1999). Student council, volunteering, basketball, or marching-band: What kind of extracurricular activity matters? *Journal of Adolescent Research, 14,* 10-43.

Eccles, J. S., Jacobs, J. E., Lanza, S., Osgood, D. W., & Wigfield, A. (2002). Changes in Children's Self-Competence and Values: Gender and Domain Differences across Grades One through Twelve. *Child Development, 73*(2), 509-527.

Eccles, J. S., Wigfield, A., MacIver, D., Reuman, D. A., & Midgley, C. (1991). Transitions During Early Adolescence: Change's in Children's Domain-Specific Self-Perceptions and General Self-Esteem Across the Transition to Junior High School. *Developmental Psychology, 27*(4), 552-565.

Eccles, J. S., A. Wigfield, C. A. Flanagan, C. Miller, D. A. Reuman, and D. Yee. (1989). Self-concepts, domain values, and self-esteem: Relations and changes at early adolescence. *Journal of Personality* 57, no. 2, 283-310.

Eder, D., & Hallihan, M. (1978). Sex Differences in Children's Friendships. *American Sociological Review, 43*(April), 237-250.

Eder, D. & Parker, S. (1987). The cultural production and reproduction of gender: The effect of extracurricular activities on peer-group culture. *Sociology of Education, 60,* 200-213.

Elliott, G. C., Kao, S., & Grant, A. (2004). Mattering: Empirical validation of social-psychological concept. *Self and Identity, 3*, 339-354.

Ensminger, M.E., Forrest, C.B., Riley, A.W., Kang, M., Green, B.F., Starfield, B., & Ryan, S.A. (2000). The validity of measures of socioeconomic status of adolescents. *Journal of Adolescent Research*, 15(3), 392-419.

Epps, E.C. (1969). Correlates of academic achievement among northern and southern urban Negro students. *Journal of Social Issues*, 1969, 25, 55-70.

Erikson, E. H. (1968). *Identity, Youth, and Crisis*. New York: Norton.

Essau, C. A. (2004). The association between family factors and depressive disorders in adolescents. *Journal of Youth and Adolescence, 33*(5), 365-372.

Fejgin, N. (1994). Participation in high school competitive sports: A subversion of school mission and contribution to academic goals. *Sociology of Sport Journal,* 11, 211-230.

Fenzel, M. L. (2000). Prospective study of changes in global self-worth and strain during the transition to middle school. *Journal of Early Adolescence, 20*(1), 93-117.

Fischer, J. L., Sollie, D., Sorell, G. T., & Green, S. K. (1989). Marital Status and Career Stage Influences on Social Networks of Young Adults. *Journal of Marriage and the Family, 51*(2), 521-534.

Flouri, E. and A. Buchanan. (2003). The role of father involvement in children's later mental health. *Journal of Adolescence* 26, 63-78.

Forehand, R., & Nousiainen, S. (1993). Maternal and paternal parenting: Critical dimensions in adolescent functioning. *Journal of Family Psychology*, 7, 213-221.

Forum of Child and Family Statistics. (2005). America's children: Key national indicators of well-being. Childstats.gov/Americaschildren.

Frank, S., Pirsch, L., & Wright, V. (1990). Late adolescents' perceptions of their relationships with their parents: relationships among deidealization, autonomy, relatedness, and insecurity and implications for adolescent adjustment and ego identity status. *Journal of Youth and Adolescence,* 19(5), 571-588.

Fredericks, J., Alfred-Liro, C., Hruda, L., Eccles, J., Patrick, H., & Ryan, A. (2002). A qualitative exploration of adolescents' commitment to athletics and the arts. *Journal of Adolescent Research,* 17, 68-97.

Freeman, H., & Brown, B. B. (2001). Primary attachment to parents and peers during adolescence: Differences by attachment style. *Journal of Youth and Adolescence,*

30(6), 653-674.

Freud, A. (1958). Psychoanalytic study of the child. *Adolescence, 15*, 255-278.

Freud, S. (1949). *An Outline of Psychoanalysis.* New York: Norton.

Furman, W., Brown, B, & Feiring, C. (1999). *Contemporary Perspectives on Adolescent Romantic Relationships.* New York: Cambridge University Press.

Furstenberg, F., Jr. (1995). Family change and the welfare of children: What do we know and what can we do about it? *Gender and Family Change in Industrialized Countries,* pp. 245-257, New York: Oxford University Press.

Furse, J. H. (2006). Belly Bomb. *New York Daily News.* (3-6-06).

Galambos, N. L., Leadbeater, B. J., & Barker, E. T. (2004). Gender differences in the risk factors for depression in adolescence: A 4-year longitudinal study. *International Journal of Behavioral Development, 28*(1), 16-26.

Garmezy, N. & Rutter, M. (1983). *Stress, Coping, and Development in Children.* New York: McGraw-Hill.

Gauze, C., Bukowski, W. M., Aquan-Assee, J., & Sippola, L. K. (1996). Interactions between family environment and friendship and associations with self-perceived well-being during adolescence. *Child Development, 67*, 2201-2216.

Gavin, L. A., & Furman, W. (1989). Age differences in adolescents' perceptions of their peer groups. *Developmental Psychology, 25*, 827-834.

Ge, X., Elder, G. H., Regnerus, M., & Cox, C. (2001). Pubertal transitions, perceptions of being overweight, and adolescents' psychological maladjustment: Gender and ethnic differences. *Social Psychology Quarterly, 64*(4), 363-375.

Gecas, V., & Schwalbe, M. L. (1986). Parental behavior and adolescent self-esteem. *Journal of Marriage and the Family, 48*, 37-45.

Gecas, V., & Seff, M. (1990). Families and adolescents: A review of the 1980's. *Journal of Marriage and the Family, 52*(November), 941-958.

Gilligan, C. (1982). *In a Different Voice,* Cambridge, MA: Harvard University Press.

Gilligan, C. (1996). The centrality of relationship in human development. In G. G. Noam & K. W. Fischer (Ed.), *Development and Vulnerability in Close Relationships,* pp.237-261. Mahwah, NJ: Lawrence Erlbaum.

Gilman, R. (2001). The Relationships between Life Satisfaction, Social Interest, and

Frequency of Extracurricular Activities Among Adolescent Students. *Journal of Youth and Adolescence, 30*(6), 749-767.

Gjerde, P. F., Block, J., & Block, J. H. (1988). Depressive symptoms and personality during late adolescence: Gender differences in the externalization- internalization of symptom expression. *Journal of Abnormal Psychology, 97*(4), 475-486.

Glasgow, K. L., Dornbusch, S. M., Troyer, I., Steinberg, L., & Ritter, P. L. (1997). Parenting styles, adolescents' attributions, and educational outcomes in nine heterogeneous high schools. *Child Development, 68*(3), 507-529.

Gold, D., & Andres, D. (1978). Developmental comparisons between ten-year old children with employed and non-employed mothers. *Child Development*, 49, 75-84.

Goodman, E., & Whitaker, R. C. (2002). A prospective study of the role of depression in the development and persistence of adolescent obesity. *Pediatrics,* 110(3), 497-504.

Goodman, E., Slap G. B., & Huang, B. (2003). The public health impact of socioeconomic status on adolescent depression and obesity. *Adolescent Health,* 93(11), 1844-1850.

Gore, S., Aseltine, R. H., & Colton, M. E. (1992). Social structure, life stress, and depressive symptoms in a high school aged population. *Journal of Health and Social Behavior,* 33, 97-113.

Gore, S., Farrell, F., & Gordon, J. (2001). Sports involvement as protection against depressed mood. *Journal of Research and Adolescence,* 11(1), 119-130.

Gould, M. S., Fisher, P., Parides, M., Flory, M., & Shaffer, D. Psychosocial risk factors of child and adolescent completed suicide. *Archives of General Psychiatry,* 53, 1155-1162.

Gould, M. S., Greenberg, T., Velting, D. M., & Shaffer, D. (2003). Youth suicide risk and preventative interventions: a review of the past 10 years. *Journal of the American Academy of Child Adolescent Psychiatry,* 42, 386-405.

Graber, J. A., Britto, P. R., & Brooks-Gunn, J. (1999). What's love got to do with it: Adolescents' and young adults' beliefs about sexual and romantic relationships. In W. Furman, B. B. Brown & C. Fiering (Eds.), *The development of romantic relationships in adolescence,* pp. 364-395. New York: Cambridge University Press.

Gray-Little, B., & Hafdahl, A. R. (2000). Factors influencing racial comparisons of self-esteem: A quantitative review. *Psychological Bulletin, 126*(1), 26-54.

Greenberg, M. T., Siegel, J. M., & Leitch, C. J. (1983). The nature and importance of attachment relationships to parents and peers during adolescence. *Journal of Youth and Adolescence,* 12, 373-386.

Grunbaum, J. A., Kann, L., Kinchen, S. A., Williams, B., Ross, J. G., Lowry, R., et al. (2002). Youth risk behavior surveillance, United States, 2001. *Morbidity and Mortality Weekly Report,* 51, 1-62.

Guerney, L., & Arthur, J. (1984). Adolescent social relationships. In R. M. Lerner & N. L. Galambos (Eds.), *Experiencing adolescence: A sourcebook for parents, teachers, and teens*, pp. 87-118. New York: Garland.

Gurian, M., & Ballew, A. C. (2003). *Boys and Girls Learn Differently.* San Francisco: John Wiley and Sons.

Hall, G. S. (1904). *Adolescence: Its Psychology and its Relations to Physiology, Anthropology, Sociology, Sex, Crime, Religion, and Education.* New York: D. Appleton and Company.

Hansen, D. M., Larson, R. W., & Dworkin, J. B. (2003). What adolescents learn in organized youth activities: A survey of self-reported developmental experiences. *Journal of Research on Adolescence,* 13(1), 25-55.

Hansford, B.C. and J.A. Hattie. (1982). The relationship between self and achievement/performance measures. *Review of Educational Research,* 52, 123-142.

Harker, K. (2001). Immigrant generation, assimilation, and adolescent psychological well-being. *Social Forces,* 79(3), 969-1004.

Harris, K. M., & P. S. Morgan (1991). Fathers, sons and daughters: Differential paternal involvement in parenting. *Journal of Marriage and the Family,* 53, 531-544.

Harter, S. (1990). Self and Identity Development. In S. S. Feldman & G. R. Elliott (Eds.), *At the Threshold: The Developing Adolescent* (pp. 352-387). Cambridge, MA: Harvard University Press.

Harter, S. (1998). The Development of self-representations. In w. a. N. E. Damon (Ed.), *Handbook of Child Psychology* (pp. 553-618). New York: Wiley.

Harter, S. (1999). *The Construction of the Self: A Developmental Perspective.* New York: Guilford.

Hartos, J. L., & Power, T. G. (2000). Relations among single mothers' awareness of their adolescents' stressors, maternal monitoring, mother-adolescent communication, and adolescent adjustment. *Journal of Adolescent Research,* 15(5), 546-563.

Hartup, W. W. (1993). Adolescents and Their Friends. In B. Laursen (Ed.), *New Directions for Child Development: Close Friendships in Adolescence* (Vol. 60, pp. 3-21). San Francisco: Jossey-Bass Publishers.

Hewitt, J. P. (1998). *The Myth of Self-Esteem*, NY: St. Martin's Press.

Heyns, B. (1982). The influence of parents' work on children's school achievement. In S. B. Kamerman & C. D. Hayes (Ed.), *Families that Work: Children in a Changing World* (229-267), Washington D.C.: National Academy Press.

Heyns, B., & Catsambis, S. (1986). Mother's employment and children's achievement: A critique. *Sociology of Education,* 59, 140-151.

Hill, J., & Lynch, H. (1983). The intensification of gender-related role expectations during adolescence. In J. Brooks-Gunn & A.C. Petersen (Ed.), *Girls at Puberty* (pp. 201-228). NY: Plenum.

Hofferth, S. L., Boisjoly, J. & Duncan, G. J. (1998). Parents' extrafamilial resources and children's school attainment. *Sociology of Education* 71, 246-268.

Hoffman, L. W. (1980). Effects of maternal employment in the two parent family. *American Psychologist*, 44, 282-292.

Hoffman, J. P., & Su, S. S. (1998). Stressful life events and adolescent substance use and depression: Conditional and gender differential effects. *Substance Use and Misuse*, 33, 2219-2262.

Hughes, M., & Demo, D. H. (1989). Self-perceptions of Black Americans: Self-esteem and personal efficacy. *American Journal of Sociology,* 95, 132-159.

Jacobs, J. E., Vernon, M. K.& Eccles, J. S. (2004). Relations between social self-perceptions, time use, and prosocial or problem behaviors during adolescence. *Journal of Adolescent Research,* 19(1), 45-62.

Jodl, K. M., Bridges, M., Kim, J. E., Mitchell, A. S., & Chan, R. W. (1999). *Relations among relationships: A family systems perspective.* In E. M. Hetherington, S. H. Henderson, & D. Reiss (Ed.), Adolescent Siblings in Stepfamilies: Family functioning and adolescent adjustment, Vol. 64. Mauldon, MA: Blackwell Pub.

Joyner, K. & Udry, R. J. (2000). You don't bring me anything but down: Adolescent romance and depression. *Journal of Health and Social Behavior,* 41(December): 369-391.

Kann, L., Kinchen, S. A., Williams, B. I., Ross, J. G., Lowry, R., Hill, C.V., Grunbaum, J., Blumson, P. S., Collins, J. L., & Kolbe, L. J. (1998). Youth risk behavior surveillance, United States, 1997. *Journal of School Health,* 68, 355-369.

Keenan, K., & Hipwell, A. E. (2005). Preadolescent clues to understanding depression in girls. *Clinical Child and Family Psychology Review,* 8(2), 89-105.

Kennedy, E. (1995). Correlates of perceived popularity among peers: A study of race and gender differences among middle school students. *Journal of Negro Education,* 64, 186-195.

Kerns, K. A., Klepac, L., & Cole, A.K. (1996). Peer relationships and preadolescents' perceptions of security in the mother-child relationship. *Developmental Psychology, 32,* 457-466.

Kidwell, J.S. (1981). Number of siblings, sibling spacing, sex, and birth order: Their effects on perceived parent-adolescent relationships. *Journal of Marriage and the Family*, 43, 315- 332.

Kilbourne, J. (1995). *Slim Hopes: Advertising and the Obsession with Thinness.* Produced, directed, and edited by Sut Jhally. Northampton, MA: The Media Education Foundation.

Kindlon, D., & Thompson, M. (2000). *Raising Cain: Protecting the Emotional Life of Boys.* New York: Ballantine Publishing Group.

Klaczynski, P. A., Goold, K. W., & Mudry, J. J. (1999). Culture, obesity stereotypes, self-esteem, and the "thin ideal": A social identity perspective. *Journal of Youth and Adolescence,* 33(4), 307-317.

Kling, K. C., Hyde, J. S., Showers, C. J., & Buswell, B. N. (1999). Gender differences in self-esteem: A meta-analysis. *Psychology Bulletin, 125*(4), 470-500.

Kohlberg, L. A. (1966). *Cognitive-Developmental Analysis of Children's Sex-Role Concepts and Attitudes.* In E.E. Maccoby (Ed.), The Development of Sex Differences, Stanford, CA: Stanford University Press

Kondo, D. (1990). *Crafting Selves: Power, Gender, and Discourses of Identity in a Japanese Workplace.* Chicago, IL: The University of Chicago Press.

Kosky, R., Silburn, S, & Zubrick, S. (1986). Symptomatic depression and suicide ideation: A comparative study with 628 children. *Journal of Nervouse and Mental Disease,* 17, 523-528.

Kowaleski-Jones, L. & Mott, F. L. (1998). Sex, contraception and childbearing among high-risk youth: Do different factors influence males and females? *Family Planning Perspectives,* 30, 163-169.

Krein, S. F., & Beller, A. H. (1988). Educational Attainment of Children from Single-Parent Families: Differences by Exposure, Gender, and Race. *Demography* 25(2), 221-234.

Laible D.J. & Carlo, G. (2004). The differential relations of maternal and paternal support and control to adolescent social competence, self-worth, and sympathy. *Journal of Adolescent Research, 19*(6), 759-782.

Lansford, J. E., Criss, M. M., Pettit, G. S., Dodge, K. A., & Bates, J. E. (2003). Friendship quality, peer group affiliation, and peer antisocial behavior as moderators of the link between negative parenting and adolescent externalizing behavior. *Journal of Research on Adolescence, 13*(2), 161-184.

Larson, R. & Richards, M. (1994). *Divergent worlds: The emotional lives of mothers, fathers, and adolescents*. NY: Basic Books.

Lasko, D. S., & Field, T. M. (1996). Adolescent depressed mood and parental unhappiness. *Adolescence, 31*(121), 5-35.

Leary, M. R., Tambor, E. S., Terdal, S. K., & Downs, D. L. (1995). Self-esteem as an interpersonal monitor: The sociometer hypothesis. *Journal of Personality and Social Psychology, 68,* 518-530.

Lempers, J. D., & Clark-Lempers, D. S. (1992). Young, middle, and late adolescents' comparisons of the functional importance of five significant relationships. *Journal of Youth and Adolescence* 21(1), 53-96.

Lerner, R. M., Sparks E., & McCubbin, L. (1999). *Family Diversity and Family Policy: Strengthening Families for America's Children.* Norwell. MA: Kluwer.

Lewinsohn, P. M., Rohde, P., & Seeley, J. R. (1996). Adolescent suicide ideation and suicide attempts: Prevalence, risk factors, and clinical implications. *Clinical and Psychological Science and Practice,* 3, 25-46.

Lewinsohn, P. M., Rohde, P., Seeley, J. R., & Kliein, D. N. (2003). Psychosocial functioning of young adults who have experienced and recovered from major depressive disorder during adolescence. *Journal of Abnormal Psychology, 112*(3), 353-363.

Little, S. A., & Graber, J. (2004). Interpersonal and achievement orientations and specific tressors predict depressive and aggressive symptoms. *Journal of Adolescent Research,* 19(1), 63-84.

Liu, Y. (2003). Parent-child interaction and children's depression: The relationships between parent-child interaction and children's depressive symptoms in Taiwan. *Journal of Adolescence, 26,* 441-446.

Liu, X., H.B. Kaplan, and W. Risser. (1992). Decomposing the reciprocal relationships between academic achievement and general self-esteem. *Youth Society, 24,* 123-148.

Lord, S. E., & Eccles, J. S. (1994). Surviving the junior high school transition. *Journal of Early Adolescence, 14*(2), 162-200.

Lundberg, S., & Plotnick, R. D. (1990). Effects of state welfare, abortion and family planning policies on premarital childbearing among white adolescents. *Family Planning Perspectives, 22*(6), 246-51, 275.

Maccoby, E. E. (1994). The role of parents in the socialization of children: An historical overview. In P. A. O. Ross D. Parke, John J. Rieser, and Carolyn Zahn-Waxler (Ed.), *A Century of Developmental Psychology*. Washington D.C.: American Psychological Association.

Maccoby, E., & Jacklin, C. (1974). *The Psychology of Sex Differences.* Stanford, CA: Stanford University Press.

Maccoby, E., & Martin, J. (1983). Socialization in the context of the family: Parent child interaction. In P. H. Mussen (Ed.), *Handbook of Child Psychology, 4,* 1-100. New York: Wiley.

McFarlane, A. H., Bellissimo, A., & Norman, G.R. (1995). Family structure, family functioning and adolescent well-being: The transcendent influence of parental style. *Journal of Child Psychology and Psychiatry and Allied Disciplines, 36*(5), 847-864.

Marcia, J. E. (1993). *Ego Identity: A Handbook for Psychological Research*. New York: Springer-Verlag.

Markstrom, C. M. (1999). Religious involvement and adolescent psychosocial development. *Journal of Adolescence, 22,* 205-221.

Markus, H.R. & Kitayama, S. (1991). Culture and the self: Implications for cognition, emotion, and motivation. *Psychological Review, 98,* 224-253.

Marini, M. M. (1990). Sex and gender: What do we know? *Sociological Forum, 5*(1), 95-120.

Marsh, H. W. (1987). Masculinity, femininity, and androgyny: Their relations with multiple dimensions of self-concept. *Multivariate Behavioral Research, 22,* 91-118.

Matsushima, R. & Shiomi, K. (2003). Social self-efficacy and interpersonal stress in adolescence. *Social Behavior and Personality, 31,* 323-33

Maton, K. (1990). Meaningful involvement in instrumental activity and well being. *American Journal of Community Psychology,* 18, 297-320.

McAdoo, H. P. (1999). *Diverse Children of Color.* In H. Fitzgerald, B. Lester, & B. Zuckerman (Eds.), Children of Color" Research, Health, and Policy Issues, pp. 205-218). New York: Garland.

McAuley, E. (1994). *Physical activity and psychosocial outcomes.* In C. Bouchard, J. Shephard, & T. Stephens (Ed.), pp. 551-568, Physical Activity, Fitness, and Health. Champaign, IL: Human Kinetics.

McDonald, G. W. (1980). Parental power and adolescents' parental identification: A reexamination. *Journal of Marriage and the Family,* May, 289-296.

McDonald, G. W. (1977). Parental identification by the adolescent: A social power approach. *Journal of Marriage and the Family,* Nov., 705-719.

McFarlane, A. H., Bellissimo, A., & Norman, G. R. (1995). The role of family and peers in social self-efficacy: Links to depression in adolescence. *American Journal of Orthopsychiatry, 65,* 402-410.

McFarlane, A. H., Bellissimo, A., & Norman, G.R. (1995). Family structure, family functioning and adolescent well-being: The transcendent influence of parental style. *Journal of Child Psychology and Psychiatry and Allied Disciplines, 36*(5), 847- 864.

McHale, S. M., Updegraff, K. A., Jackson-Newsom, J., Tucker, C. J., & Crouter, A. C. (2000). When Does Parents' Differential Treatment Have Negative Implications for Siblings? *Social Development, 9*(2), 149-172.

McNeal, R.B. (1999). Parental involvement as social capital: Differential effectiveness on science achievement, truancy, and dropping out. *Social Forces*, 78(1), 117-144.

Mead, G. H. (1934). *Mind, Self, and Society.* Chicago: University of Chicago.

Mechanic, D., & Hansell, S. (1987). Adolescent competence, psychological well-being, and self-assessed physical health. *Journal of Health and Social Behavior* 28, 364-374.

Mechanic, D., & Hansell, S. (1989). Divorce, family conflict, and adolescents' well-being. *Journal of Health and Social Behavior, 30,* 105-116.

Metz, S. L. (1995). *The Relationship Between Parental Behaviors and Children's Self-*

Esteem. Nebraska: The University of Nebraska.

Mikulincer, M. (1998). Adult attachment style and individual differences in functional versus dysfunctional experiences of anger. *Journal of Personality and Social Psychology,* 74(2), 513-524.

Miller, L., & Merav, G. (2002). Religiosity, depression., and physical maturation in adolescent girls. *Child & Adolescent Psychiatry,* 41(2), 206-214.

Mirowsky, J. (1996). Age and gender gap in depression. *Journal of Health and Social Behavior, 37,* 362-380.

Montgomery, M. (2005). Psychosocial intimacy and identity: From early adolescence to emerging adulthood. *Journal of Adolescent Research,* 20, 346-374.

Mulkey, L. M., Crain, R. L., & Harrington, A. J. (1992). One-parent households and achievement: Economic and behavioral explanations of a small effect. *Sociology of Education* 65, 48-65.

Muller, C. (1995). Maternal employment, parental involvement, and mathematics achievement among adolescents. *Journal of Marriage and the Family,* 57(1), 85-100.

Nada, R. R., McGee, R., & Stanton, W. (1992). Perceived attachment to parents and peers and psychological well-being in adolescence. *Journal of Youth and Adolescence, 21,* 471-485.

National Institute of Mental Health. (2000). *Depression in children and adolescents.* Bethesda, MD: Department of Health and Human Services.

National Longitudinal Study of Adolescent Health (Add Health). (2003). http://www.cpc.unc.edu/addhealth. Chapel Hill, NC: UNC Carolina Population Center.

Needham, B. L., & Crosnoe, R. (2005). Overweight status and depressive symptoms during adolescence. *Journal of Adolescent Health,* 36(1), 48-55.

Nielsen, L. (2001). Fathers and daughters: Why a course for college students? *College Student Journal, 35*(2), 280-317.

Nolen-Hoeksema, S. (1987). Sex differences in unipolar depression: Evidence and theory. *Psychological Bulletin,* 101, 259-289.

Nolen-Hoeksema, S., & Girgus, J. S. (1994). The emergence of gender differences in depression during adolescence. *Adolescence, 115*(3), 424-443.

Nolen-Hoeksema, S., Girgus, J. S., & Seligman, M. E. (1991). Sex differences in depression and explanatory style in children. *Journal of Youth and Adolescence, 20*, 233-245.

Noom, M. J., Dekovic, M., & Meeus, W. H. J. (1999). Autonomy, attachment an psychological adjustment during adolescence: A double-edged sword? *Journal of Adolescence, 22*, 771-783.

Nottleman, E. D. (1987). Competence and self-esteem during transition from childhood to adolescence. *Developmental Psychology, 23*(3), 441-450.

Ogletree, M. D., Jones, R. M., & Coyl, D. D. (2002). Fathers and their adolescent sons: Pubertal development and paternal involvement. *Journal of Adolescent Research, 17*(4), 418-424.

O'Koon, J. (1997). Attachment to parents and peers in late adolescence and their relationship with self-image. *Adolescence, 32*(126), 471-483.

Ouellet, R., & Joshi, P. (1986). Loneliness in relation to depression and self-esteem. *Psychological Reports, 58*, 821-822.

Owens, T. J. (1994). Two dimensions of self-esteem: Reciprocal effects of positive self-worth and self-deprecation on adolescent problems. *American Sociological Review, 59*(3), 391-407.

Papini, D. R., & Roggman, L.A. (1992). Adolescent perceived attachment to parents in relation to competence, depression, and anxiety: A longitudinal study. *Journal of Early Adolescence, 12*, 420-440.

Parcel, T., and Meneghan, E. (1993). Family social capital and children's behavior problems. *Social Psychology Quarterly*, 56.

Parker, S., Nichter, M., Nichter, M., Vuckovic, N., Sims, C., & Ritenbaugh, C. (1995). Body image and weight concerns among Afincan Americana and White adolescent females: Differences that make a difference. *Human Organization, 54*, 103-114.

Parson, T. (1964). Social Structure and Personality. NY: Free Press of Glencoe.

Paterson, J., Field, J. & Pryor, J. (1994). Adolescents' Perceptions of their Attachment Relationships with their Mothers, Fathers, and Friends. *Journal of Youth and Adolescence, 24*, 579-600.

Paxton, S. J., Wertheim, E. H., Gibbons, K.,Szmukler, G. I., Hillier, L, & Petrovich, J. L. (1991). Body image satisfaction, dieting beliefs, and weight loss behaviors in adolescent boys and girls. *Journal of Youth and Adolescence, 20*, 361-379.

Pesa, J. A., Syre, T. R., & Jones, E. (2000). Psychosocial differences associated with body weight among female adolescents: The importance of body image. *Journal of Adolescent Health,* 26, 330-337.

Pett, M. A., Vaughan-Cole, B., & Wampold, B. E. (1994). Maternal Employment and Perceived Stress. *Family Relations,* 43, 151-158.

Phinney, J. S., Cantu, C. L., & Kurtz, D. A. (1997). Ethnic and American identity as predictors of self-esteem among African American, Latino, and White adolescents. *Journal of Youth and Adolescence,* 26(2), 165-185.

Phinney, J. S., & Devich-Navarro, M. (1997). Variations in bicultural identification among African American and Mexican American adolescents. *Journal of Adolescent Research,* 7, 3-32.

Pike, A., & Plomin, R. (1996). Importance of nonshared environmental factors for childhood and adolescent psychopathology. *Journal of the American Academy of Child and Adolescent Psychiatry,* 35, 560-570.

Pine, D. S., Cohen, E., Cohen, P., & Brook, J. (1999). Adolescent depressive symptoms as predictors of adult depressive: Moodiness or mood disorder? *American Journal of Psychiatry,* 156, 133-135.

Pipher, M. (1994). *Reviving Ophelia: Saving the Selves of Adolescent Girls.* New York: Putnam.

Portes, A. (2000). The two meanings of social capital. *Sociological Forum,* 15(1), 1-12.

Quatman, T., & Watson, C. M. (2001). Gender differences in adolescent self-esteem: An exploration of domains. *Journal of Genetic Psychology,* 162(1), 93-118.

Radziszewska, B., Richardson, J.L., Dent, C.W., & Flay, B.R. (1996). Parenting style and adolescent depressive symptoms, smoking, and academic achievement: Ethnic, gender, and socioeconomic status differences. *Journal of Behavioral Medicine,* 19(3), 289-305.

Raja, S. N., McGee, R., & Stanton, W. R. (1992). Perceived attachment to parents and p peers and psychological well-being. *Journal of Adolescence,* 21, 471-485.

Rey, J. M. (1995). Perceptions of poor maternal care are associated with adolescent depression. *Journal of Affective Disorders,* 34, 95-100.

Renk, K., & Creasey, G. (2003). The relationship of gender, gender identity, and coping strategies in late adolescents. *Journal of Adolescence,* 26, 159-168.

Ridgeway, C. L. (1997). Interaction and the conservation of gender inequality: Considering employment. *American Sociological Review,* 62, 218-235.

Ridgeway, C. L. (2001). Gender, status, and leadership. *Journal of Social Issues,* 57(4), 637-655.

Roberts, R. E. L., & Bengtson, V. L. (1993). Relationships with parents, self-esteem, and psychological well-being in young adulthood. *Social Psychology Quarterly,* 56(4), 263-277.

Roberts, J. E., Gotlib, I. H., & Kassel, J. D. (1996). Adult attachment security and symptoms of depression: The mediating roles of dysfunctional attitudes and low self-esteem. *Journal of Personality and Social Psychology,* 70(2), 310-320.

Robinson, R. B., & Frank, D. I. (1994). The relations between self-esteem, sexual activity, and pregnancy. *Adolescence,* 29(113), 13-26.

Rohrbaugh, J., & Jessor, R. (1975). Religiosity in youth: A personal control against deviant behavior. Journal of Personality, 43, 136-155.

Rosenberg, M. (1965). *Society for Adolescent Self-Image*. Princeton, NJ: Princeton University Press.

Rosenberg, M. (1986, 1979). *Conceiving the Self*. Melbourne, FL: Krieger.

Rosenberg, M., & McCullough, B. C. (1981). *Mattering: Inferred significance and mental health among adolescents*. In R. Simmons (Ed.) Research in community and mental health (Vol. 2, p. 163-182). Greenwich, CT: JAI Press.

Rosenberg, M., & Pearlin, L. I. (1978). Social class and self-esteem among children and adults. *American Journal of Sociology,* 84(1), 53-77.

Rosenberg, M., Rosenberg,F., & Simmons, R. G. (1973). Disturbance in the self-image at adolescence. *American Sociological Review,* 54, 1004-1018.

Rosenberg, M., Schooler,C., & Schoenbach, C. (1989). Self-esteem and adolescent problems: Modeling reciprocal effects. *American Sociological Review*, 38(5), 553-568.

Ross, C. E., & Broh, B. A. (2000). The roles of self-esteem and the sense of personal control in the academic achievement process. *Sociology of Education,* 73, 270-284.

Ross, C. E., & Huber, J. (1985). Hardship and depression. *Journal of Health and Social Behavior,* 26, 312-327.

Rotheram-Borus, M. J., Dopkins, S., Sabate, N., & Lightfoot, M. (1996). Personal and ethnic identity, values, and self-esteem among Black and Latino adolescent girls.

In B. J. R. L. a. N. Way (Ed.), *Urban Girls: Resisting Stereotypes, Creating Identities* (Vol. 35-52). New York: New York University Press.

Rubin, L. B. (1984). *Intimate Strangers: Men and Women Together*. New York: Harper & Row.

Russell, A., Pettit G.S., and Mize, J. (1998). Horizontal Qualities in Parent-Child Relationships: Parallels with and Possible Consequences for Children's Peer Relationships. *Developmental Review,* 18, 313-352.

Salmons, P.H., & Harrington, R. (1984). Suicidal ideation in university students and other groups. *The International Journal of Social Psychiatry*, 30, 201-205.

Sartor, C. E., & Youniss, J. (2002). The Relationship Between Positive Parental Involvement and Identity Achievement During Adolescence. *Adolescence,* 37(147), 221-234.

Savin-Williams, R. C. & Demo, D. H. (1984). Developmental change and stability in adolescent self-concept. *Developmental Psychology,* 20, 1100-1110.

Schapman, A. M., & Inderbitzen-Nolan, H. M. (2002). The role of religious behaviour in adolescent depressive and anxious symptomatology. *Journal of Adolescence,* 25, 631-643.

Schmidt, J. A., & Padilla, B. (2003). Self-esteem and family challenge: An investigation of their effects on achievement. *Journal of Youth and Adolescence,* 32(1), 37-46.

Schneider, B. H., Atkinson, L. & Tardiff, C. (2001). Child-parent attachment and children's peer relations: A quantitative review. *Developmental Psychology,* 37(1), 86-100.

Schwartz, S. J., & Montgomery, M. J. (2002). Similarities or differences in identity development? The impact of acculturation and gender on identity process and outcome. *Journal of Youth and Adolescence,* 31(5), 359-372.

Seff, M. A., Gecas, V., & Ray, M. P. (1992). Injury and Depression: The Mediating Effects of Self-Concept. *Sociological Perspectives,* 35(4), 573-591.

Shaffer, D., Gould, M. S., Fisher, P., Trautman, P., Moraeu, D., Kleinman, M., et al. (1996). Psychiatric diagnosis in child and adolescent suicide. *Archives of General Psychiatry* 53(4): 339-348.

Shanahan, M. J., Finch, M., Mortimer, J. T. & Ryu, S. (1991). Adolescent work experience and depressive affect. *Social Psychological Quarterly* 54(4), 299-317.

Simons, R.L., & Murphy, P.I. (1985). Sex Differences in the Causes of Adolescent

Suicide Ideation. *Journal of Youth and Adolescence,* 14, 423- 434.

Simmons, R. G., & Rosenberg, F. (1975). Sex, sex roles, and self-image. *Journal of Youth and Adolescence,* 4, 229-258.

Simmons, R. G., Rosenberg, F., and Rosenberg M. (1973). Disturbance in the self-image at adolescence. *American Sociological Review,* 38, 553-568.

Smith, E. J. (2002). The Black female adolescent: A review of educational, career and psychological literature. *Psychology of Women Quarterly,* 6, 261-288.

Smith, H. M., & Betz, N. E. (2002). An examination of efficacy and esteem pathways to depression in young adulthood. *Journal of Counseling Psychology, 49,* 438-448.

Smoll, F., & Smith, R. (1989). *Children and Youth in Sport: A biopsychosocial perspective.* Chicago, IL: Brown & Benchmark.

Smucker, M. R., Craighead, W. E., Craighead, L. W., & Green, B. J. (1986). Normative and reliability data for the Children's Depression Inventory. *Journal of Abnormal Child Psychology,* 14, 25-39.

Soares, A. T., & Soares, L. M. (1969). Self-perceptions of culturally disadvantaged children. *American Educational Research Journal,* 6, 31-45.

Son, S. E., & Kirchner, J. T. (2000). Depression in Children and Adolescents. *American Family Physician,* 62(10), 2297-2308.

Sorenson, S. B., Rutter, C. M., & Aneshensel, C. S. (1991). Depression in the community: An investigation into age of onset. *Journal of Consulting and Clinical Psychiatry, 59,* 541-546.

Sprock, J., & Yoder, C. Y. (1997). Women and depression: An update on the report of the APA task force. *Sex Roles,* 36, 269-303.

Stack, S. (1983). The effect of the decline in institutionalized religion on suicide, 1954-1978. *Journal for the Scientific Study of Religion,* 22, 239-252.

Stanley, K. D., & Murphy, M. R. (1997). A comparison of general self-efficacy with self-esteem. *Genetic, Social, and General Psychology Monographys,* 123, 79-99.

State of California. (1986). *A bill to establish California commission to promote self-esteem and personal and social responsibility, Sept. 23.* Sacramento: State of California.

Steelman, L. C., Powell, B., Werum, R. & Carter, S. (2002). Reconsidering the Effects of Sibling Configuration: Recent Advances and Challenges. *Annual Review of*

Sociology, 28, 243-269.

Steinberg, L. (2001). Adolescent development. *Annual Review of Psychology, 52*, 83-110.

Steinberg, L., Elmen, D. J., & Mounts, N. S. (1989). Authoritative parenting, psychosocial maturity, and academic success among adolescents. *Child Development, 60*, 1424-1436.

Steinberg, L. (1987). Recent research on the family at adolescence: The extent and nature of sex differences. *Journal of Youth and Adolescence*, 16(3), 191-197.

Stevenson, H. & Stigler, J. (1992). *The Learning Gap*, New York: W.W. Simon & Schuster.

Stright, A. D., & Bales, S. S. (2003). Coparenting quality: Contributions and parent characteristics. *Family Relations, 52*(3), 232-249.

Sullivan, H. S. (1953). *The Interpersonal Theory of Psychiatry*, New York: W.W. Norton & Company.

Sun, Y., & Li, Y. (2001). Marital disruption, parental investment, and children's academic achievement: A prospective analysis. *Journal of Family Issues, 22*(1), 27-62.

Surtees, P. G., Wainwright, N.W., & Pharoah, P. D. (2002). Psychosocial factors and sex differences in high academic achievement at Cambridge University. *Oxford Review of Education*, 28(1), 21-38.

Symister, P., & Friend, R. (2003). The influence of social support and problematic support on optimism and depression in chronic illness: A prospective study evaluating self-esteem as a mediator. *The American Psychological Association, 22*(2), 123-129.

Taylor, G. J., Bagby, G. J., & Parker, J. D. A. (1997). *Disorders of affect regulation: Alexithymia in medical and psychiatric illness*. Cambridge, MA: Cambridge University Press.

Taylor, J. & Turner, R. J. (2001). A Longitudinal Study of the Role and Significance of Mattering for Depressive Symptoms. *Journal of Health and Social Behavior, 42*, 309-324.

Thorne, B. (1997). *Gender Play*. New Brunswick, NJ: Rutgers University Press.

Thornton, A., Orbuch, T. L., and Axinn, W. G. (1995) "Parent-Child Relationships During the Transition to Adulthood." *Journal of Family Issues*, 16(5), 538-564.

Tucker, C. J., McHale, S. M., & Crouter, A. C. (2003). Dimensions of mothers' and fathers' differential treatment of siblings: Links with adolescents' sex-typed personal qualities. *Family Relations, 52*(1), 82-98.

Tracy, A. J., & Erkut, S. (2002). Gender and race patterns in the pathways from sports participation to self-esteem. *Sociological Perspectives, 45*(4), 445-466.

Udry, J. R. (2003). The *National Longitudinal Survey of Adolescent Health, Wave I.* Chapel Hill: Carolina Population Center, University of North Carolina.

Umana-Taylor, A. J., Diversi, M., & Fine, M. A. (2002). Ethnic identity and self-esteem among Latino adolescent: Distinctions between Latino populations. *Journal of Adolescent Research, 17*(3), 303-327.

United States Bureau of the Census. (1996). *Children by presence of siblings by type of relationship and race and ethnicity.* Survey of Income and Program Participation.

United States Bureau of the Census. (2003). Washington D.C.: Government Printing Office.

United States Bureau of the Census. (2006). *Household relationship and living arrangements of children under 18 years.* Current Population Survey, 2006 Annual and Economic Supplement.

University of Michigan Depression Center. (2006). http://www.med.umich.edu/depression/programs.htm.

Usmiani, S. & Daniluk, J. (1997). Mothers and their adolescent daughters: Relationship between self-esteem, gender role identity, and body image. *Journal of Youth and Adolescence, 26,* 45-62.

Veneziano, R. A. (2000). Perceived paternal and maternal acceptance and rural African American and European American youths' psychological adjustment. *Journal of Marriage and the Family, 62,* 123-134.

Verkuyten, M. (2003). Positive and negative self-esteem among ethnic minority early adolescents: Social and cultural sources and threats. *Journal of Youth and Adolescence, 32*(4), 267-277.

Videon, T. M. (2002). Who plays and who benefits: Gender, interscholastic athletics, and academic outcomes. *Sociological Perspectives, 45*(4), 415-444.

Wade, T. J. (1991). Race and Sex Differences in Adolescent Self-Perceptions of Physical Attractiveness and Level of Self-Esteem During Early and Late Adolescence. *Personality and Individual Differences, 12,* 1319-1324.

Warner, V., Weismann, M. M., Mufson, L., & Wickramaratne, P. J. (1999). Grandparents, parents, and grandchildren at high risk for depression: a three-generational study. *Journal of the American Academy of Child and Adolescent Psychiatry,* 38, 289-296.

Way, N. (1995). "Can't you see the courage, the strength that I have?": Listening to urban adolescent girls speak about their relationships. *Psychology of Women Quarterly*, 19: 107.

West, C., & Zimmerman, D. H. (1991). Doing gender. In J. L. a. S. A. Farrell (Ed.), *The Social Construction of Gender* (pp. 13-37). Newbury Park, CA: Sage.

Whitaker, A., Davies, M. D., Shaffer, J., Johnson, S., Abrams, B. T., Walsh, T., & Kalikow, K. (1989). The struggle to be thin: A survey of anorexic and bulimic symptoms in a non-referred adolescent population. *Psychological Medicine*, 19, 143-163.

Whitbeck, L. B., Simons, R. L., Conger, R. D., Lorenz, S. H., & Elder, G. H. (1991). Family economic hardship, parental support, and adolescent self-esteem. *Social Psychology Quarterly*, 54(4), 353-363.

Whitbeck, L. B., Conger, R. D., & Kao, M. (1993). The influence of parental support, depressed affect, and peers on the sexual behavior of girls. *Journal of Family Issues,* 14, 261-278.

Whitbeck, L. B., Hoyt, D. R., Miller, M., & Kao, M. (1992). Parental support, depressed affect, and sexual experience among adolescents, *Youth & Society,* 24, 166-177.

White, M. J., & Glick, J. E. (2000). Generation status, social capital, and the routes out of high school. *Sociological Forum*, 15(4), 671-691.

Whitley, B. E. (1983). Sex role orientation and self-esteem: A critical meta-analytical review. *Journal of Personality and Social Psychology*, 44, 765-778.

Wichstrom, L. (1999). The emergence of gender difference in depressed mood during adolescence: The role of intensified gender socialization. *Developmental Psychology,* 35, 232-245.

Wilkinson, R. B. (2004). The role of parental and peer attachment in psychological health and self-esteem of adolescents. *Journal of Youth and Adolescence,* 33, 479-493.

Wong, E., Wiest, D. J., & Cusick, L. B. (2002). Perceptions of Autonomy Support, Parent Attachment, Competence and Self-Worth as predictors of Motivational Orientation and Academic Achievement: An Examination of Sixth and Ninth Grade Regular Education Students. *Adolescence,* 37(146), 255-267.

World Health Organization. (1999). http://www.who.int/en.

Wulff, M. B., & Steitz, J. A. (1999). A path model of the relationship between career indecision, androgyny, self-efficacy, and self-esteem. *Perceptual and Motor Skills, 88,* 935-940.

Yarrow, M. R., Scott, P., de Leeuw, L., & Heinig, C. (1962). Child-rearing in families of working and nonworking mothers. *Sociometry,* 25(2), 122-140.

Youniss, J. & Smollar, J. (1985). *Adolescents Relations with mothers, fathers, and friends.* Chicago: University of Chicago Press.

Zhang, J, & Jin, S. (1996). Determinants of suicide ideation: A comparison of Chinese and American college students. *Adolescence,* 31(122), 451-468.

Zimmerman, P. (1999). Structure and functions of internal working models of attachment and their role for emotion regulation. *Attachment and Human Development,* 1(3), 291-306.

APPENDIX

Complete listing of variable survey questions/statements and answer choices.

A. Symptoms of Depression (National Institute of Mental Health, 2006)

1. Persistent sad, anxious, or "empty" mood
2. Feelings of hopelessness, pessimism
3. Feelings of guilt, worthlessness, helplessness
4. Loss of interest or pleasure in hobbies and activities that were once enjoyed
5. Decreased energy, fatigue, being "slowed down"
6. Difficulty concentrating, remembering, making decisions
7. Insomnia, early-morning awakening, or oversleeping
8. Appetite and/or weight loss or overeating and weight gain
9. Thoughts of death or suicide; suicide attempts
10. Restlessness, irritability
11. Persistent physical symptoms that do not respond to treatment, such as headaches, digestive disorders, and chronic pain

B. Adolescent Depressed Mood (Wave I and Wave II)

Q: How often was each of the following true during the last week?
A: *never or rarely, sometimes, a lot of the time, most of the time or all of the time*

1. You were bothered by things that usually don't bother you.
2. You didn't feel like eating, your appetite was poor.
3. You felt that you could not shake off the blues, even with help from you family and your friends.
4. You felt that you were just as good as other people.
5. You had trouble keeping your mind on what you were doing.
6. You felt depressed.
7. You felt that you were too tired to do things.
8. You felt hopeful about the future.
9. You thought your life had been a failure.
10. You felt fearful.
11. You were happy.
12. You talked less that usual.
13. You felt lonely.
14. People were unfriendly toward you.
15. You enjoyed life.
16. You felt sad.
17. You felt that people disliked you.
18. It was hard to get started doing things.
19. You felt that life was not worth living.

C. Adolescent Self-Esteem (Wave 1 and Wave 2)
   Q: How much do you agree with the following statements?
   A: *strongly disagree, disagree, neither agree nor disagree, agree, strongly agree*

   1. you have a lot of good qualities
   2. you have a lot to be proud of
   3. you feel like you are doing everything just about right
   4. you feel socially accepted
   5. you feel loved and wanted
   6. you like yourself just the way you are

D. Parental Educational Attainment
   Q: How far did your mother/father go in school?

   1. never went to school
   2. eighth grade or less
   3. more than eighth grade but did not graduate from high school
   4. went to business, trade, or vocational school instead of high school
   5. high school graduate
   6. completed a GED
   7. went to business, trade, or vocational school after high school
   8. went to college but did not graduate
   9. graduated from a college or university
   10. professional training beyond a four-year college or university

E. Adolescent Participation in School Clubs
   Q: Which activities do you currently participate in or plan to participate in the coming school year?

   1. French club
   2. German club
   3. Latin club
   4. Spanish club
   5. Book club
   6. Computer club
   7. Debate club
   8. Drama club
   9. Future Farmers of America
   10. History club
   11. Math club
   12. Science club
   13. Band
   14. Cheerleading/dance team
   15. Chorus or choir

16. Orchestra
17. Newspaper
18. Honor Society
19. Student council
20. Yearbook
21. Other club or organization

F. Adolescent Participation in School Athletics

Q: Which activities do you currently participate in or plan to participate in the coming school year?

1. Baseball/ softball
2. Basketball
3. Field Hockey
4. Football
5. Ice hockey
6. Soccer
7. Swimming
8. Tennis
9. Track
10. Volleyball
11. Wrestling
12. Other sport

Wissenschaftlicher Buchverlag bietet

kostenfreie

Publikation

von

wissenschaftlichen Arbeiten

Diplomarbeiten, Magisterarbeiten, Master und Bachelor Theses
sowie Dissertationen, Habilitationen und wissenschaftliche Monographien

Sie verfügen über eine wissenschaftliche Abschlußarbeit zu aktuellen oder zeitlosen Fragestellungen, die hohen inhaltlichen und formalen Ansprüchen genügt, und haben **Interesse an einer honorarvergüteten Publikation**?

Dann senden Sie bitte erste Informationen über Ihre Arbeit per Email an info@vdm-verlag.de. Unser Außenlektorat meldet sich umgehend bei Ihnen.

VDM Verlag Dr. Müller Aktiengesellschaft & Co. KG
Dudweiler Landstraße 125a
D - 66123 Saarbrücken

www.vdm-verlag.de